British Library Cataloguing in Publication Data.
A catalogue record for this publication is available from the British Library.

For more information:
Visit our website for more Practice Exam Questions and answers.
www.sociologyzone.co.uk
Email us for further information:
info@sociologyzone.co.uk

About the Exam Notes

Written with examination success in mind!

- These exam notes have been written by Sociology examiners and experienced teachers, with only one purpose in mind — **exam success**. Using these exam notes will help students achieve the best possible grade in their Sociology exam.

- We have provided the depth of information required for your Sociology examinations, both in terms of knowledge and evaluation, which makes these exam notes more concise than general Sociology text books, and more comprehensive than standard revision guides (which often lack the depth of evaluation required to achieve an A grade).

We have focused on the 'evaluation' part.

- Contrary to popular belief, learning and memorising lots of facts and theories will not get you a grade A or B in your exam. The exam requires you to be able to 'analyse' and 'evaluate' sociological knowledge, this does not mean jotting down a few brief criticisms at the end of your essay. The analysis and evaluation that you make, needs to be expanded upon and explained in an effective manner. With this in mind, we have written a lot of the evaluation points using the three-steprule: identify, expand and conclude. We have done this for you in this book to demonstrate what a 'developed' evaluation point looks like. Please try and remember this technique and demonstrate it in your exam.

Practice Exam Questions

- We have given you lots of Practice Exam Questions at the end of each exam note to practise. We have covered most of the different types of questions you may be asked for each topic both at AS and at A Level. If you are taking the A level course, it is a good way of testing and practising both your knowledge and examination skills. You may realise some of the questions require the same answers, but are worded differently, this was deliberate, just so you are familiar with the different way the questions can be worded.

- Please visit www.sociologyzone.co.uk for exam notes, Practice Exam Questions, mark schemes, model answers and much more.

Contents

Section 1

Beliefs in Society

AQA Specification

Beliefs in Society	**AQA**
Students are expected to be familiar with sociological explanations of the following content:	• ideology, science and religion, including both Christian and non-Christian religious traditions • the relationship between social change and social stability, and religious beliefs, practices and organisations • religious organisations, including cults, sects, denominations, churches and New Age movements, and their relationship to religious and spiritual belief and practice • the relationship between different social groups and religious/spiritual organisations and movements, beliefs and practices • the significance of religion and religiosity in the contemporary world, including the nature and extent of secularisation in a global context, and globalisation and the spread of religions

The AQA specification:
- Different theories of religion

The exam requires that you are able to:
► Describe the functionalist theory of religion.
► Evaluate the functionalist theory of religion.

Introduction

To functionalists, religion is an important part of society as it helps integrate people together by sharing common beliefs, morals, and opinions. This creates a value consensus in society (people sharing the same values).
By sharing the same values this unites people together and creates social solidarity/cohesion in society. It is important for individuals to co-exist in society in a harmonious way otherwise without integration society can be prone to breaking down and falling into disorder and conflict. As such religion helps maintain the same values and social norms held collectively by all in society which is important for maintaining social control and order in society.
Therefore, the contribution of religion in society and to the individual is both positive and beneficial.

Durkheim and Religion

Durkheim's famous publication 'Elementary Forms of Religious Life' (1912), analyses the role and function of religion based on secondary sources collected by anthropologists on the small primitive Aboriginal Arunta tribe in Australia (Durkheim had never visited the small tribe). Durkheim focused on researching a primitive tribe because he believed that by studying this basic form of religion which has not been manipulated by man, he hoped to gain insights and apply his findings to more sophisticated religious systems (e.g. Christianity).

- **Totem.** Durkheim points out that members of the tribe would often worship a totem (e.g. object such as plant, animal carving) which is seen as sacred symbol by the group. The existence of an *external object* like the totem is an important one, as this allows rituals and ceremonies such as collective worshipping to take place. This helps integrate the group together and reinforce the tribe to their shared identity. This ultimately provides a sense of belonging within their community.

- **Sacred and the profane.** Durkheim found that the *totem*, places and other rituals were viewed by the tribe as being sacred (reverences or having a special meaning) and anything that was not connected to the totem was seen as *profane* – that is not sacred, such as everyday activity that does not have any religious significance or meaning. The distinction between the sacred and profane is an important one because the sacred allows its members to come together and celebrate collectively. This creates a collective conscience; the sharing of the same beliefs, morals, values, opinions. This is important, because if individuals are left to their own for a long amount of time, without sacred objects being at the centre of the group, the beliefs and convictions of the group will weaken, whereas sacred object helps reinforce the collective conscience.

- **Worshipping of society.** Durkheim argues that the tribe as a 'group' exists because of the totem. The collective worship around the totem is really the worshipping of the tribe itself. The worshipping towards the sacred objects is not really towards the object itself as such, but must mean something more significant. He claims that its members are really (unconsciously) *worshipping their own social group's identity*.

Malinowski: Psychological Function
- **In times of uncertainty/risk.** Malinowski's (1954) theory on the role of religion was based on a study of a small-scale tribal society in the Trobriand Islands. In studying the Trobriand Islanders, Malinowski found that fishing in

the lagoon was not preceded by rituals (no risk) but fishing in the open sea, amid conditions of uncertainty and risk, was always preceded by rituals. This led him to believe that religion helps provide security and *explanations* in times of uncertainty and crisis (unpredictable or uncontrollable events) e.g. death, illness, unemployment etc. Religious explanations help produce confidence and a feeling of control in times of crisis and fear.

- **Anomie.** Parsons (1965) argues that religion helps deal with 'life crisis' which would otherwise lead to **anomie** (break down of norms of behaviour) that can threaten the stability and order in society. Religion gives meaning to ultimate questions (e.g. life after death) and to the meaningless and inexplicable suffering and evil (e.g. cancer in babies). Belief in concepts such as immortality, heaven, funeral ceremonies, helps in the stability of a healthy society, as it provides meaning to such events.

Parsons: Reinforcing Core Values

- **Parsons** (1965) argues that one function of religion is to reinforce the core values of society and that religion helps make them sacred (e.g. not stealing, or committing adultery, murder) which helps re-affirm society's social values. This helps promote social stability and order in society. For example, the Ten Commandments in the bible reinforces the social values. The commandment 'thou shalt not commit adultery' demands that families stay together, thus reinforcing social cohesion. 'Thou shalt not steal' refers to the respect for private properties, a religiously respected societal value.

Bellah: Civil Religion

- **Civil religion.** Robert Bellah (1970) on the analysis of American society argues that the religious beliefs will eventually die as society becomes more secular and more diversified. However, he argues that certain social activities perform the same functions of uniting people together just like religion has done, which he calls *civil religion*. These are non-religious events, in which people are united by a faith in their shared nationalism which is expressed through ritual, ceremonies and beliefs (e.g. royal weddings, memorial days, flag waving, and national team sport) which help integrate its members in society in a similar way to that of religion. This unity of society can be achieved by civil religion.

✓✗ Evaluation

> **✓ Conflict theories**
>
> Marxists and feminists accept the functionalist view that religion can promote social stability. *However*, they offer a differing perspective in that they do not see it as beneficial for society as a whole. Marxists see religion as benefiting the ruling class, whereas feminists see religion; benefiting a patriarchal society, reinforcing the status quo of men. This suggests that the functionalist view of religion is partially correct according to feminists and Marxists but would disagree on the outcome.

> **✓ Rise of new religions and fundamentalism**
>
> There is empirical evidence to support the functionalist view of religion. The growth of new religious movements across the globe proves that religion is a universal necessity, and thus in a sense it could be argued that it is functional as people need religion. Also, the rise of extreme fundamentalism could be seen as a reaction to the weakening of society's norms and values in a postmodern world, and may be a response to the threat of anomie in today's society.

> **✗ Postmodernists**
>
> Postmodernists argue that functionalists view religion as less significant in modern multi-cultural societies, where a diverse range of religious beliefs and practices mean religion can no longer play the role of uniting and integrating people as did in a traditional society with one monotheistic faith. This would suggest that the functionalist view is no longer valid in a modern diverse society.

✗ Rise in new age movements

The growth of new age movements suggest that people have become disillusioned by institutional faiths, as they may no longer provide an adequate explanation and security, as suggested by Malinowski and Parsons. People now seek other forms to help with life crisis, such as emphasis on spirituality, self-healing and personality improvement therapies. This would suggest that the functionalist view that mainstream religion provides meaning and emotional support in a modern society may to some extent no longer be valid.

✗ Religion can bring conflict

Religion can be a source of conflict and tension within a society. For example, the conflict in Northern Ireland between the Protestants and Catholics, or in Iraq between Shia and Sunni Muslims. In the UK, rising tensions of Muslim communities can often lead to conflict and culture clashes e.g. Bradford riots. Or between societies such as the Arab-Israeli conflict in Palestine, Iran-Iraq war in the 80s. This shows that the function of religion does not always unit and integrate its members but that it can at times be dysfunctional for society.

✗ Methodological flaws in Durkheim's research

Durkheim only studied a small number of Aboriginal tribes which meant that; a) his sample was small making it non-representative and therefore hard to generalise his findings to society as whole; b) there is also the issue of applying his study of a primitive tribe to a large diverse modern society; c) finally, his research findings are based on secondary sources not on first hand evidence, therefore giving rise to errors, bias and misinterpretation. Such methodological issues question the validity of his research findings, and thus his theories as it is based on such research evidence.

✗ Methodological flaws in Malinowski research

Malinowski's study was carried out in the 1950's on a small scale non-literate Trobriand Islanders which means that the research findings are non-representative and not applicable to modern complex industrialised societies. Again such methodological issues question whether we can generalise the research findings beyond the tribe the research was based upon.

✗ Religion can be psychologically damaging

The functionalist view ignores the potential psychological damage religion can have on people. The concept of damnation, sin, and hell can often leave people, especially young children, feeling anxious and terrified. Religious laws that are broken can often evoke feelings of fear, guilt, and low self-esteem in people and in some cases lead to people committing suicid.

Exam Questions

1. Outline and explain **two** functions in which religion can play in society . . . . **[10 marks]**

2. Outline and explain **two** limitations of the functionalist view of religion . . . . **[10 marks]**

3. Applying material from **Item...** and your knowledge, evaluate the claim that religion brings about harmony and consensus. . . . . **[20 marks]**

4. Applying material from **Item...** and your knowledge, evaluate the claim that religion is more likely to be a source of conflict than of cohesions. . . . . **[20 marks]**

The AQA specification:
- Different theories of religion

The exam requires that you are able to:
▶ Describe the Marxist theories of religion.
▶ Evaluate the Marxist theories of religion.

Introduction

Marxists see capitalist society as made up of two classes: the ruling class (bourgeoisie) and the working class (proletariat). The ruling class own the means of production (companies, factories, shops) which generates a wealthy income. The working class being the labour force, are exploited by the ruling class keeping wages as low as possible in order to maximise the profit of the ruling class. This creates a conflict between the two classes. Marxist believed that the working class will eventually be aware of their exploitation and rise up to overthrow the ruling class and replace capitalism with a classless society where everyone is equal and exploitation is removed (utopian society). However, religion prevents this from occurring and helps continues to reinforce a class divided society.

Marxism and Religion

Marxists disagree with functionalist that religion benefits the whole of society. Marxist see the role of religion as an important one that benefits the ruling class. **Religious ideology** can be effective method of **social control** over the working-class; the ruling class controlling and maintaining power over the working class without using physical force. This results is that working class are less likely to challenge their status quo and revolt against the ruling class, and thus religion can be seen as benefiting the interests of the ruling class. Religion serves the interest of the ruling class by:

- **Distort reality.** Religion blinds the working class of understanding their real reason for their poor situation; being exploited by the ruling class. Explanation of that inequality has been justified by religious ideas (e.g. sin, God's providence, God works in mysterious way, the after-life). Religious ideas distort how working class people view reality; By distorting their view, this creates a **false class-consciousness** amongst the working class as it helps them accept their position as the norm.

- **Religion legitimises class inequality.** Religion justifies inequality between the classes as being fair and natural because it has been ordained by God as expressed in the religious hymn *"All things bright and beautiful': "The rich man in his castle, the poor man at his gate, God made them, high or lowly, and ordered their estate".* Religion also reduces the chance of revolt through the concept of 'hell'. Those who do evil will be damned in hell; such a concept creates the fear of hell amongst the working class and minimises any challenges made to existing social order as this would be a direct challenge to God.

- **The opiate of the masses.** Karl Max saw religion as the 'opium for the people' By this he meant that religion 'drugs' the working class by providing comforting diversion from seeing and attacking the real cause of their poverty (i.e. the injustice of capitalist system) by promising eternal happiness in the afterlife, this helps the working class people to accept their poverty on earth because of the potential rewards in the afterlife are huge. Marx saw as the illusion of happiness after death. Such an illusion, helps maintain and sustain the social inequality between the classes.

Supporting empirical evidence

Empirical evidence to support the Marxist view of religion:

- **Class inequality.** The Hindu caste system in India encourages social class divisions. This hierarchical religious system determines before birth which social position people will be born in society ('Brahmins' being the highest and 'untouchables', the lowest position). The caste system will determine the job to which one can aspire to in life, and as a result will determine their socioeconomic status in society.

- **Religious faith is strongest amongst the poor.** The growth of religious belief is often found to be strongest among the poor, the oppressed and the working class, especially amongst women who are the least powerful in society. This may explain the growth of Islam and the veiling of Muslim women in some of the poorer regions in the Middle East (Afghanistan, Iraq, Palestine and Iran).

✓✗ Evaluation

✓ Feminism

Aspects of the Marxist theory of religion is supported by feminists. They would agree with Marxism view that religion can act as a form of social control against the working class. However, they would go further and argue that religions are oppressive especially towards women, because religion is used to justify a patriarchal society.

✓ Functionalism

Marxist and functionalists would agree that religion acts as a form of social control but they differ in whom benefits from this. To the functionalist, it regulates and maintains social order which is good for the stability of society as a whole. To the Marxist, it prevents the working class from realising their true position in society — one of exploitation and oppression.

✓ Religious faith is strongest amongst the poor

The growth of religious belief is often found to be strongest among the poor, the oppressed and the working class, especially amongst women, who are the least powerful in society. This may explain the rise in the veiling of Muslim women in some of the poorer regions in the Middle East such as in Afghanistan, Iraq, Palestine and Iran for example. This seem to show that Marxist theory may have validity as it is supported by empirical evidence.

✗ Religion helps the poor

Neo-Marxists claim that religion does not always act in a controlling manner against the working class. They believe that religious organisations have often taken the side of the oppressed working class against the injustices of capitalism. For example, Father Camilo Torres in the 1960s, is a real life example of a Colombian Catholic priest who practised liberation theology by becoming a guerrilla fighter against the corrupt government, in order to liberate the marginalised and ill-treated working class from poverty and exploitation of capitalism. In this way, religion was used to influence the type of economic society to a fairer and just system.

✗ Secularisation issue

The process of secularisation has meant that religious beliefs and religious worshipping have declined in some western societies. This means religious ideology acting as a form of controlling factor may no longer be applicable if people don't believe in religion any more. This suggest that Marxist theory of religion may not be as valid in modern western societies.

✗ Methodological issues

Some of Marxist's concepts are difficult to research to see if they are true. For example, the idea of a 'false consciousness', what type of research would be carried out to test this concept? How will the variable 'false consciousness' be operationalised and measured? (process of converting the variables in a way that can be tested and measured in practical terms). What would the researcher be looking for? This makes some of the concepts impossible to prove or disprove, which makes the Marxist theory of religion unscientific.

✗ Postmodernist

Marxists have been criticised by postmodernists. They argue that recent fragmentation of beliefs (reflected in the growth of many NRMs and NAMs) has weakened the influence religion has over people. Individuals can reason for themselves, and can pick and choose the aspects of religion which they find appealing. This suggest that it is hard to see how people are manipulated by religion, as suggested by Marxists.

Exam Questions

1. Outline and explain **two** limitations of the Marxist view of religion. . . . . **[10 marks]**

2. Applying material from **Item...** and your knowledge, evaluate the claim that religion performs an ideological function in the interest of powerful groups. . . . . **[20 marks]**

The AQA specification:
- Different theories of religion

The exam requires that you are able to:
▶ Describe the Feminist theories of religion
▶ Evaluate the Feminist theories of religion.

Introduction

Feminism see society as being patriarchal—male-dominated. As a result, they see religious institutions are patriarchal which is used to benefit and support males mainly two ways:

○ Religious belief and teachings reinforce gender inequality.

○ Religious belief and teachings are used to legitimates female subordination in society (e.g. family, motherhood roles)

Below are examples feminists use to demonstrate the patriarchy of religion:

- **Place of worship.** Miller and Hoffmann (1995) found that although women are far more likely than men to attend collective worship and to do so regularly, women are segregated from males, when it comes to worshipping (Islam and Orthodox Judaism), as not to distract them. Muslim women and Jewish Orthodox women are also prohibited from reading their holy scriptures (the Koran and the Torah respectively) or participating in symbolic rituals and festivals or enter the place of worship when menstruating (Islam).

- **Gender differences in images of God.** Feminists claim that men have 'masculinised' religious characters, and the important figures are primarily males, which implies that God prefers their gender characteristics. For example, in the Old Testament it says that man was made 'in the image of and to the glory of God', whereas women were made 'for the glory of man'. In the Old and New Testaments, as well as the Koran, the most important prophets are male (e.g. Isaiah, Moses); again, all the disciples of Jesus were men. Feminists claim that males tend to play down the important role of females in religious texts, such as the roles of Eve, Mary mother of Jesus, and Mary Magdalene.

- **Women in religious organisations.** El Saadawi (1980) argues that religious organisations mainly male dominated. For example, it is noted that high-status positions within traditional religions tend to be given to men. Orthodox Jews, the Catholic Church, the Orthodox Church and Islam continue to exclude women from the religious hierarchy. Although she argues that monotheistic faiths are not in themselves patriarchal, the fact that men have written, dominated and interpreted religion throughout history has led to the suppression of women. However, recently some religions such as the Church of England and the Anglican Church, as well as some liberal synagogues have now made an effort to allow women to take up positions of authority.

- **Female body.** De Beauvoir (1949) argues that the female body in religious scriptures are often portrayed in a negative way, evil or a temptress, leading men astray. Such representation in religious teaching has led to the control and subordinate of women in religions and society. For example:

- *Women are seen as temptress.* In Islam, women worship separately from men as they are viewed as a distraction. Women are asked to adhere to a restrictive dress code, such as veiling among some Islamic women, so as not to invite male lust. In the Christian story of creation (in 'Genesis'), Eve is portrayed as being responsible for the creation of sin on earth through eating the forbidden apple from the tree of knowledge.

- *A male possession.* Women are seen as male possessions in mainstream religions. For example, in traditional weddings the nearest male relative (usually the father) of the bride is asked to 'give her away'. Saadawi (1980) argue that in some Islamic traditions, young females are required to undergo female mutilation in order to control their sexual behaviour thus reducing the likelihood that she will become sexually active with anyone other than her husband (and thus remain a virgin until she is married).

- *Control of female identity.* some feminists see the Islamic veil as a form of social control, denying the freedom of women to express their gender identity. Veiling further supports the notion that women's sexuality is seen as a sinful distraction for men.

Fundamentalism, NRMs and women

- **Fundamentalism.** The rise of fundamentalism in some religions (such as Islam) has attempted to reinforce the traditional view of women in society, and also in terms of their domestic role of housewife. Cohn and Kennedy (2000) argue that female autonomy has been associated with fear, as it could undermine the foundations of the family, religion, morality and the dominance of male control. For example, fundamentalist groups in Afghanistan, Iran, Iraq, Turkey and Pakistan have tried ruthlessly to reinstate women's traditional role.

- **NRMs.** New Religious Movements (NRMs) and New Age Movements (NAMs) have seen a rise in membership, particularly of women members. Bruce (1995) claims that the ratio of female:male involvement is 2:1. According to Bruce, they are particularly attractive to women because they are non-hierarchical, less domineering, less confrontational, and more co-operative and caring. Such religious movements may themselves reflect the more equal greater female status in today's society compared to 30 years ago.

✓✗ Evaluation

✓ Marxism

Marxists would agree with feminists that religion acts as an agent of social control. They both see religion as an instrument to maintain the subordinate position of women Where they differ is that Marxism sees religion as benefiting the ruling class, whereas feminists see it as benefiting men. This shows that the feminist theory has similarities and is supported with other critical perspectives on religion.

✗ Functionalists

Feminism has been criticised by functionalists. This is because functionalists argue that that patriarchal society and religion does not necessarily mean the oppression of women. Patriarchal societies and religions allow different roles for women and men to suit their 'nature' and are therefore 'natural' and functional for society. They also argue that feminists ignore the benefits that religion can have for women: religion can provide both psychological, spiritual and mental stability for many women; it offers meaning and understanding, especially in times of crisis.

✗ Freedom to choose

Some sociologists have questioned the 'passive' role suggested by feminists. Badawi (1994) argues that women now have much choice over their interpretation of their religion. For example, Muslim women in Turkey have the freedom to choose whether to be veiled (wear a headscarf) or not.

✗ Women in religious positions

Not all religions can be criticised for being patriarchal. Recent evidence has shown that women are now taking up positions of authority in religions, especially in the Christian Pentecostal and Anglican churches, and the Church of England has allowed female vicars since 1992. Alexandra Wright argues that Reformed Judaism has allowed women to become rabbis since 1972. Arguably, Buddhism have never been oppressive to women. This would suggest that the feminist approach is not applicable to all religion, and is losing some grounds in modern society.

✗ Open to interpretation

Butler (1990) has questioned the feminist view that religion is seen as a form of social control. She interviewed young Muslim women in Britain, and found that veiling was a source of identity amongst women, showing their cultural and religious roots, rather than a symbol of oppression. This is supported by Watson (1994) see the veiling of Islamic women as a liberating force. It reduces the possibility of sexual harassment and allows women to be judged as people, rather than on what they look like. She also concludes that veiling is a reaction against secular values and western culture; it has taken on a new meaning, becoming a symbol that signifies a rejection of western values, not a symbol of social control.

Exam Questions

1. Outline and explain **two** reasons why women are no longer oppressed by religion.. . . . . **[10 marks]**

2. Applying material from **Item…** and your knowledge, evaluate the feminist contribution to the understanding of religion in contemporary society. . . . . **[20 marks]**

The AQA specification:

- The relationship between social change and social stability, and religious beliefs, practices and organisations

The exam requires that you are able to:

► Describe how do sociological theories explain the relationship between religions and social change.
► Evaluate these sociological explanations.

Key terms

- Religion as a **conservative force** means two things:

  ○ *Maintain existing order of society.* Religion operates to inhibits changes to occur society and to maintain the existing social order of society— 'conserve' how thing are.
  Examples: maintaining a patriarchal society, segregated domestic family roles.

  ○ *To conserve traditional customs.* Religion as a conservative force means keeping the traditional customs, beliefs and morals. (which can often mean reverting to traditional and values from the past)
  Examples: Catholicism and orthodox Christianity forbid abortion, divorce and artificial contraception.

- Religion as a **social change** means:

  ○ *Bring about changes in society.* Religion can be used as a force for social changes in society. For example, laws on abortion, or more radical changes such as the Islamic revolution in Iran, orchestrated by Ayatollah Khomeini, a religious leader who brought about a social change from a pro-western-government-led society to an Islamic republic.

The debate

- The relationship between religion and social change is complex and should never been seen as straightforward. Sociologists have debated whether religion can be used as instrument to bring about social change in society, or whether the role of religion is primarily a conservative one, to maintain social order—inhibits change. Functionalism, Marxism and feminism see the role of religion as a conservative force (i.e. preventing social change), although for different reasons. Other sociologists, take a historical analysis as well as modern examples, suggest that religion has led people or groups to seek changes in society using religion as instrument for social change.

Religion as a conservative force

Functionalist view: religion as a conservative force

- **Durkheim.** Functionalists support the view that religion operates as a conservative force. According to Durkheim this is because, religion promote people in society to share the same traditional value and norms know as **value consensus** and also **social solidarity** amongst the people in society. Having behaviour that 'chime' together towards values and norms (known as **collective consciousness**), this helps keep social order and social control in society. so in this respect religion can operate as a conservative force. Durkheim argues that deviation from the agreed norms and values that religion teaches is seen as negative and dysfunctional for society, that can bring about social change.

- **Parsons** elaborates further Durkheim view, and suggests that role of religion is to discourage deviant behaviour by putting in place written down codes of ethics which provides moral guidance. The 10 commandments are written as a constant reminder that social rules must be obeyed so that social solidarity is maintained. For example, "thou shall not steal" makes private property and meritocracy become accepted societal values that have been religiously endorsed.

Marxist: religion as a conservative force

- Marxists agree with functionalists in that religion can operate as conservative force, but for different reasons. Functionalists see this as beneficial for society, whereas Marxists see it as negative. Religion is used to perpetuate class inequality. Religion is used as an ideological state apparatus, which creates false class consciousness in working class people; fooling the working class into believing that society is equal and fair. According to Marxists, religion functions as a drug because it 'opiate the people', into seeing the world as it really is – one of exploitation and suppression. According to Marxists, religion is a tool used by the ruling class as an instrument of social control; it maintains the subordinate position of the working class in society. Therefore, religion operates as a conservative force maintaining social order through false class consciousness and stopping revolutionary thought of overthrowing capitalism society. For example, hard work is necessary to gain gods favour is a central belief in most religious doctrines e.g. in the afterlife.

Feminist view: religion as a conservative force

- Feminists also agree with functionalists and the Marxist point of view. De Beauvoir (1949) argue that religion is used as an instrument to maintain the existing patriarchal society. They see religion as being used and manipulated by man to control and oppress women in most areas of life, such as family and religious life, as it is religious 'holy men' (vicars, imams) who translate sacred texts to their followers. De Beauvoir (1949) claims women in religious organisations often play a secondary role, with no real position of religious power or hierarchical importance. This shows that religious organisations reinforce gender inequality, which stops society accepting women as equals and therefor, religion inhibits social change and preservers the status quo.

Religion as a force for social change

Social action theorist: religions as force for change

- Weber was a social action theorist, who claimed that religion can lead to social change. His attempts to explain why capitalism was unique to 19th Century Western civilisation. Weber (1905) in *The protestant ethic and the spirit of capitalism*, attempts give a reason for this: it was the religious beliefs of Calvinists (a form of Protestant Christianity) that lead to the development of capitalism in Western societies. Calvinist Protestants were responsible for social change and the creation of capitalism in two ways:

  - *Protestant ethics* – the Calvinist belief system suggested that man was an instrument of God. This meant that correct way to carry out God's will, is to work a vocation and to abstain from social or leisure time as this was frowned upon. This disciplinarian austere approach to work and life was known as the 'protestant ethic.' According to Weber, this was the main reason that brought about a social change from small scale cottage industry to mechanised industrial production, as any extra wealth was reinvested rather than spent on luxury items.

  - *Pre-destination* – a second reason why Calvinism led to social change was through belief in predestination. This concept meant that God selected certain people for a place in heaven at birth (pre-determined), known as the 'elect'. and nothing they did in their lives could change the outcome. Since no one could be sure if they were the chosen ones, Weber argues that this prompted what he called 'salvation-anxiety'. The 'signs' of successful selection for a place in heaven were possibly demonstrated by having a 'successful businesses and an austere and discipline lifestyle. According to Weber, Calvinist values of commitment to hard work led to social change because other people had to compete with heaven-backed hard work.

- The combination of the two points above was the reason for the growth and development for capitalism in western countries. Such 'work ethics' brought growth to business investments, which in turn was reinvested back into business to generate more wealth and thus eventually gave rise to the growth of capitalism. According to Weber, the Calvinists belief structures were responsible for the creation of capitalism and modern society.

Neo-Marxist: religions as force for change

- Neo-Marxism shares many ideas with traditional Marxism, however there is disagreement over the role of religion in society. Otto Maduro (1982), a neo-Marxist, argues that religion can act as a force for social change in society. He accepts that in many cases the churches often support the ruling party and acts as a conservative force. However, he argues that in certain countries such as Latin America, South Africa and Poland, the Priests often practised liberation theology (a Christian doctrine) which criticises the capitalist class for the lack of help towards the working class for their suffering and social injustice that stems from capitalism. Such clergy, preach liberation theology to urge the working-class to rise and fight against the existing right wing dictators to bring about social change, the belief that religion can change the working class's oppressive situation.

Fundamentalism a force for social change

- Social change. Religious fundamentalism can be seen equally as a conservative force and a force for social change. Fundamentalist groups often want a return back to fundamental values based on a belief in a pure interpretation of religious texts and that society should be restored to its traditional form. In this way fundamentalist religious movements operate as a force for social change favouring a more fundamental, religious way of life that controls all parts of life. For example, the Isis, the Islamic fundamentalists in Syrian and Iraq seek a traditional Islamic patriarchal system based on a strict moral code of behaviour, or Christian fundamentalists who take the commandment "thou shall not kill" literally are anti-abortion and react by burning abortion clinics in US hospitals.

- Conservative force. Once fundamentalists have achieved the goal of forcing everybody to live by their religious codes then they become a conservative force. Fundamentalists seek tight control over the individual ideology through control of norms and values. In this respect, fundamentalists act as a conservative force. For example, ISIS require women in to cover themselves completely and they may not leave their homes. Children are not permitted to study art, music, natural history, literature or any religion other than Islam. Children are segregated into boys' classes and girls' classes and may only be taught by teachers of the same sex.

Factors making religion conservative or bringing about social change

- MacGuire (1981) suggests that there are a number of factors that need to be taken into consideration in order to decide whether religion can prevent or promote social change:

  - *The nature of beliefs.* Religions that adopt a strong moral code of behaviour, often produce members who will react to social inequalities in society and attempt to change it. For example, Martin Luther King's campaign for black civil rights in America in the 1960's.

  - *How significant religion is to society's culture.* When religious organisations remain central to the culture they will have an influential voice in justifying social changes or preventing it. For example, in South Africa Archbishop Desmond Tutu was a prominent opponent of apartheid.

  - *The extent of social involvement of religion.* In society where religious leaders are close connected to other influential figures that have influence of political, economic and social matters more likely to bring about social change. For example, the militant Islamic Palestinian movement Hamas was elected in January 2006 as the Palestinian Authority.

  - *Internal organisation.* Religious organisations that are central to government politics, can have an impact in bringing about social change or prevent it. For example, Cypriot Archbishop Makarios, was elected as the Greek national leader to fight British colonial rule.

✓✗ Evaluation

Religion as a conservative force

> **✗ Functionalism and Marxism not applicable to multi-cultural societies**
>
> The Marxist and functionalist views that religion acts as a conservative force has been criticised because their accounts are outdated, as they fail to account for the diversity of religious organisations in modern multi-cultural societies. With the many varying beliefs, such as the UK it is difficult to see how religion can be seen as a conservative force, if not every ascribed to the same religious beliefs and values. Marxism and functionalist views were more applicable in the 60's, when society was more homogenous, but may not be valid in today's society.

> **✗ Functionalisms and Marxism outdated**
>
> A further criticism of functionalism and Marxism is that in Britain the conservative force argument is somewhat outdated. According to Barker Western Europe is going through a 'gentle secularising process'. Religion is committed to by 10% of Britain's population. Therefore, any arguments that societal norms and values are affected by religion seem to be overestimating religions dwindling power.

> **✗ Feminists view criticised**
>
> Religion has brought about some changes in women's position in religious organisations, e.g. ordained female priests are now accepted in the Church of England, and some do not condemn homosexual practices.

Religion as a force for change

> **✓ Weber's social action theory has empirical support**
>
> Marshall (1982) argues that Weber's assumptions of Calvinism creating capitalism as being correct. Marshall goes on to argue that in any situations where Calvinism failed to produce capitalism there were a number of good reasons why this was the case. In Scotland although the Calvinists provided a base for capitalism they lacked the skilled workforce to fully develop industry.
>
> This would suggest that there is some validity to Weber's theory.

> **✓ Neo-Marxism has empirical support.**
>
> A strength of the Neo-Marxist view on relgions and social change it that have empirical support. Camilo Torres Restrepo (1929 –1966) was a Colombian Roman Catholic priest who practised liberation theology when he tried to reconcile neo-Marxism with Catholicism. He actively supported the cause of poor people and the working class, and took up arms against the ruling party, becoming a member of the National Liberation Army (ELN) guerrilla group. Camilo Torres believed that in order to secure justice for the people, Christians had a duty to use violent action to liberate the working class and the poor.

> **✗ Weber's view of capitalism criticised**
>
> Weber's social action to support the idea that religion can be social change lacks research evidence. Evidence shows that Calvinism was strong in certain countries in Europe such as Sweden, Norway and Scotland, but they did not develop into industrial capitalist societies until much later, suggesting that Calvinism was not the cause of capitalism. This would suggest that Weber's theory must be treated with a degree of caution.

✗ Capitalism proceeded Calvinism

There is research evidence that refutes Weber's view that religion bring social change. Eisenstadt (1967) argues that initially capitalism flourished in Catholic countries such as Italy, Belgium and Germany, before the protestant reformation (before the Protestant religion developed from Catholicism). This would suggest that Weber's theory may lack validity.

✗ Neo-Marxism criticised.

Neo-Marxist theory on religion and social has been criticised by mainstream Marxism. They would agree that liberation theology may have been effective in helping to bring about democracy (from military dictatorship in South America). However, Marxist would argue that liberation did have any real effect on remove capitalism, which is the cause of real social inequality.

✗ Poor theological interpretation

Weber's social action theory has been criticised because his interpretation of Calvinism as a religion could be wrong. Many Calvinist preachers taught that wealth was a great danger and provided great temptation for those that acquired it. Therefore, it seems unlikely that Calvinists would use economic success to be the benchmark that measured their acceptance into heaven. This suggests that the social action theory only offers a partial view on how religion functioned within society.

Exam Questions

1. Applying material from **Item...** analyse **two** ways arguments in support of the idea that religion is a conservative force. . . . . **[10 marks]**

2. Applying material from **Item...** and your knowledge, evaluate the claim that religion may encourage rather than inhibit social change. . . . . **[20 marks]**

The AQA specification:

- The significance of religion and religiosity in the contemporary world, including the nature and extent of secularisation in a global context, and globalisation and the spread of religions

The exam requires that you are able to:

▶ Describe the causes of secularisation globally.
▶ Evaluate the evidence for the view that secularisation is occurring.

Key terms

- **Religiosity** deals with how religious a person is by looking at belonging (identification and membership to a religion organisation), behaving (attendance to religious service) and believing in God (Clements, 2015).

- **Secularisation** is the decline of religious influence in society and in people's behaviour. Bryan Wilson (1966) defined secularisation as "the decline of the influence of religious institutions, thinking and practices upon social life".

The debate

- The secularisation debate is about whether secularization is occurring or not. Some sociologists argue claims that religiosity is declining; society and people place less importance of religion in their lives, and therefore religion is losing it influence, (known as 'secularization theorist'). Others argue against that the view that secularisation is taking place. And that religion still plays a significant role to play in society, with some suggesting a religious revival occurring showing high levels or religiosity The reason why it is a contentious issue, is the 'evidence' used to measure a person's religiosity is open to different interpretation as you will see throughout this revision notes

Secularisation in the UK

Statistical evidence

One area to exam if secularisation is occurring is looking at statistical evidence that focus on church attendance, marriages, baptism, church membership and religious beliefs, Official statistics on religion are collated from various official surveys such as the British Social Attitudes Survey, YouGov and the Census show the current importance placed on religion by the British population in modern society.

Evidence for secularisation occurring

- **Church attendance.** Statistics show that religion attendance is declining. According to figures from *UK Church Statistics (2015)*, in 1980, 11.1% (approx. 5 million) of the UK population, attended Church on a Sunday. By 2005 this dropped down to 6.3% (just over 3 million). By 2015, the level of church attendance in the UK this has fallen to just under 5% (less than 3 million). Church marriages and baptism have also seen a decline (1970 = 65%; 2015=30%). Less than half of all marriages now take place in church, favouring of civil ceremonies.

- **Affiliation.** Statistics are useful to show the decline of people being affiliated with a religious organisation A person's religious affiliation refers to their membership or identification with a religion. According to the British Social Survey (2014) one in three (31%) in 1983 did not belong to a religion and in 2015 with one in two (50%) of the UK's population do not regard themselves as belonging to a particular religion. This shows that secularisation is happening as fewer people are willing to believe and practise institutional forms of religion and therefore religion is losing its significance to individuals.

- **Age bias.** There is also an age bias in church attendance and membership. The average age of a church-goers tends (55-60 years) to be much older than those who do not attend. The older, more religious, generations are dying out and are being replaced by less religious generations. There is little evidence that substantial numbers find religion as they get older. The implication is that fewer and fewer young people are attending church which could mean that religious attendance could possibly die out altogether in years to come.

- **Beliefs.** Statistical evidence also that over 80 years, religious beliefs have been declining. According to YouGov (2105) approximately 32% of the UK population believe in a God. Polls from the younger generation (18-to 24 year olds) beliefs in a God show a lower rate of up to 25%. This suggest that religious beliefs are declining, with the younger generation having more secular views, which would imply that more people will eventually be atheist then believers.

✓✗ Evaluation

Issue of reliability and validity

Critics argue that statistical evidence are not an accurate measurement of patterns of religiosity; they should also not be used to make comparisons between the present and the past. This is mainly due to:

> ✗ **Historical evidence unreliable**
>
> In the past, there were no organised and systematic methods of gathering data across religious organisations in Europe, especially amongst the churches faiths. It was based on estimations; no opinion polls or surveys were carried out in the past to measure the pattern of religiosity over time.

> ✗ **Validity questioned**
>
> Engels suggests in the 1840's working class people had little interest in religion and regular attendance at church was not particularly high. This was despite the fact that most people who attended churches did so for social reasons as opposed to religious conviction. Hamilton (2001) argues that the past was no more religious then today, and the present secularisation debate is based on the assumption that there was a 'golden age' of a 'fully religious society'. This is incorrect; past statistical evidence shows consistently low levels of church attendance spanning over 400 years. This would imply that the empirical data from historical records needs to be treated with great caution as it lacks reliability and validity.

> ✗ **Today's data collection not standardised.**
>
> Even today, there are no real standardised ways of collecting data on membership and attendance. Each religious organisation has different criteria. Some may use membership affiliation while others will measure religiosity based on attendances during services. For example, Catholic Church may measure how many people attend Mass on a Sunday and during Easter and Christmas services rather than based on church formal electoral roll membership, whereas the Anglican Church uses the electoral roll of membership. There is also the problem of religious organisation exaggerating the numbers of attendance, or they may base This means that the evidence of quantitative may not be an accurate measure of the extent secularisation is occurring.

> ✗ **Believing without belonging**
>
> Opinion polls suggest as YouGov (2015) found that 52% of British adults believe in God or a greater spiritual power, while 14% don't know what they believe in. This seems to show that people are by nature still religious although they choose not to attend institutional worshipping. Bellah (1996) argues that there has been a move from collective to privatised worshipping and from the need for a clerical interpretation to an individual interpretation of religious doctrine. Davie (2002) calls this 'believing without belonging'. However, Voas (2013) shows that surveys consistently show religious beliefs is declining at a much faster rate then attendance.

✗ Other beliefs systems on the increase

The statistics evidence show that there is only decline in the popularity of traditional churches in the UK. Brierley (1998) compilation of statistical evidences shows that other major religions such as Sikhs and Muslims and new religious movements such as the Jehovah's Witnesses are gaining members. This would suggest that statistics only show a partial picture of secularisation in modern society in the UK.

Explanations Why Secularisation is Occurring
Below are explanations offered for the causes of secularisation.

Differential thesis
Wilson (1976) argues for the differential thesis- a process whereby the church, prior to industrialisation had political power and control over social, education, and the morality of the population, but due to industrialisation and the development of modern society, this has meant that the political and social issues are now taken over by specialised institutions. This has led to the disengagement of religion from the state and wider society; a progressive distancing of the institutions of secular society (government, education etc) from religious organisations. This means religions have little influence to control or dictate or influence secular policies on human behaviour. The differential thesis argues that religious is in decline because:

- **Decline of traditional communities.** Industrialisation has caused the shift from being tight-knit communities, to urbanised communities that are fragmented which are made up of different beliefs and values— cultural diversity. This means that the Churches can no longer serve as the focal point for local communities. Furthermore, the different variety of religious beliefs that people are exposed to, may also question the validity of their own faith.
- **Structural differentiation.** The church has gone through a process of structural differentiation. This means during the development of an industrial society, non-religious state agencies have now taken over certain functions, what were once dominated by the church. For example, the Welfare state now looks after the poor and the NHS looks after the sick. Parson (1965) argues that structural differentiation, leads to disengagement; people turn to other places other than religion, which may explain why religion has become less important in people's lives.
- **Social differentiation.** Wilson (1982) argues the church has gone through a process of social differentiation. The church has lost it influence over social issues. For example, if a person has marital problem, they may now see a marriage counsellor rather than a clergyman. As a result, according to Wilson, "religion is relegated to the margins of society where it 'ceases to be a significant in the working of the social system (Wilson, 1982).

✓✗ Evaluation

✓ Empirical evidence.

There is empirical evidence to support social differentiation thesis. Religious views on abortion, homosexuality, divorce and Sunday shopping tend to be ignored by the government now and tend not to influence social policies. In term of moral behaviour, church weddings make up only 30% of marriages compared to 75% 30 years ago; within the frame work of increasing divorce rates, and increases in cohabitation and children born outside marriage, this evidence shows disengagement is occurring, religion exercises little moral influence on people any more.

✗ Structural differentiation criticised

The structural differentiation thesis has been criticised by Parson (1965). He argues the liberation from the other functions of education, law and politics means the church to concentrates now more effectively on spiritual and moral matter such as meaning of life, death, evil and suffering. Parson argues that the success of religion answering these questions has resulted in the continuing commitment of people holding onto their faith and providing a moral compass, values consensus which is important for social order and stability in society.

Woodhead (2008) argues that Churches still play a major role during national celebration and mourning rituals, such as the wedding and death of Diana princes of Wales and the Queen Mother. The British legal system is still underpinned by religion for example, through swearing an oath on the bible. Christianity still has an influence on people' lives, such as Easter and Christmas holidays and festivities. This shows that religion although it lost its less significant non-religious functions, it is now able to specialise in matters which are still important for people in society, demonstrating religion has not become disengaged from the people in modern society.

✗ **De-privatisation**

Casanova (1994) criticised the view that religion has been become disengaged from society. In fact, he argues that religion has gone through a process of *de-privatisation*; in which religion has left the private (personal lives) to enter more prominently in the public sphere. This means religion plays an important role for society as a whole, and it still remains important in the political sphere, as in the conflict in the Middle East between the Jews and Muslim, or Isis in Syria, or the New Right Christians in the USA. This would suggest that disengagement explanation may lack validity.

Rationalisation

Rationalisation (also known desacrilisation) refers to the increasing importance of scientific explanations of the living world. Supernatural forces are no longer seen as controlling the world—supernatural meanings and the power of mystery no longer play a part.

- **Scientific and technological explanations.** Bruce (1995) argues scientific and technological explanations have replaced religious explanations of modern life. Issues which were once religious are now more likely to be dealt with by scientists, technology, psychotherapists, doctors etc. Bruce argues we no longer use natural remedies or religion to cure illness, instead we go to the doctors. This suggests that religious explanations have become obsolete; science is much more beneficial to people's immediate lives.

- **Disenchantment.** Rationalisation as evidence for secularisation has support from Weber (1976). He argues that the rise of capitalism and technological advancement brought in an era of rationality, which has brought about the diminished significance of religion in society. According to Weber, the world has been demystified; people will no longer believe in mystery and magic; the supernatural will be taken over by more intellectual explanations based on science. Weber used the term *'disenchantment'* instead of 'secularisation'.

✓✗ Evaluation

✗ **Statistical evidence question rationality explanation**

There is statistical data that refutes the claim that secularisation is occurring due to rationalisation. According to YouGov survey, (2015), just under 40% of adults in the UK believe that there is life after death, even though there is no scientific evidence that this there is. Another survey by the Institute of Education (2012), found 49% of people believed there is 'definitely' or 'probably' life after death, suggesting that people still believe in supernatural/religious explanations even in a modern rational society.

Pluralism

Religious pluralism refers to the increasing number of sects and denominations, which are found now in modern society. The rise of religious pluralism in the UK means that the Church is being replaced by many other religious organisations; there is no longer one common faith in society. Religious pluralism has contributed to the process of secularisation because array of different beliefs may challenge the Church's version of religious truths. Bruce (2002) argues that the many competing religious organisations have reduced the power of mainstream religion in modern society. This is because plurality has brought about relativism—all beliefs are seen to be seen as acceptable truths. People no longer feel controlled by the religion they are born into, as there are alternative way of thinking and behaving.

Cultural defence and transition

- Many of the 'newer' religions (e.g. Islam, Hinduism, Judaism and branches of Christianity) in Britain have been imported into the country as a result of immigration. Amongst these groups, evidence of religiosity seems to contradict the secularisation is occurring. For example:

  o Membership of religions such as Islam and Hinduism are increasing rather than declining.

  o Amongst many Afro-Caribbean groups, membership of some Christian denominations and sects remains high (for instance, Pentecostalism and Evangelicalism).

The evidence would go against the secularisation theory, however, Bruce (2002) argues that religion remains strong in society because of its social rather than religious reasons. Such as:

  o *Cultural Defence.* Religion of often used as a 'focal point' or a 'defence mechanism' to preserve the ethnic group's identity (values and traditions) when faced with hostility and conflict from a dominating culture. This may explain the high level of support for Islam among young British Pakistanis, Arabs and Africans (e.g. girls wearing the 'hijab') who will often use their faith as a cultural identity in reaction against western foreign policy in the Middle East, and in rejection of western secular values. This suggest that some religions may be on the increase for non-religious reasons, rather than for deep beliefs in their faith.

  o *Cultural Transition.* Religion is used as a resource for migrant group facing changes and adjustments such as moving to a new country or culture that threaten their identity. Religious organisation provides a sense of community and support that helps people to cope with the changes.

✓✗ Evaluation

Secularization in a global context

Critics of the secularisation thesis have argued that it can be criticised as ethnocentric, firstly for only concentrating on the dominant Christian faith, and secondly for only considering Britain. When we apply the 'secularisation debate' in other countries it becomes less-clear cut; with many showing no evidence of secularisation occurring.

Europe (Christianity)

- **Secularisation occurring in Europe.** Secularisation is clearest in some European countries. Evidence from the Eurobarometer survey (2010) conducted since 1970 suggest consistent erosion in church attendance experienced across the 15 European Union member states during the last three decades, with a fairly steep fall found in Belgium, Luxembourg and the Netherlands, pattern particularly marked among the younger generations.

- **Not in all European countries.** Despite gradually declining religious attendance in most European countries, a distinction needs to be drawn between them. For example, in the Catholic Church in Ireland, Italy, Portugal and Poland, the attendance rate remains strong, with the churches still playing an active role in social issues such as homosexuality, abortion and divorce. Countries with the Christian Orthodox faith, such as Greece, Cyprus and Romania, also show strong attendance rates.

Middle East (Islam)

- **Islam growing not declining.** Research shows that Islam is the fastest growing religion in the world. It will become the world largest religion in the world. By 2050, Muslims will be nearly as numerous as Christians, and if trends continue, Islam's population could surpass Christianity by 2100 (Pew Research Centre, 2015). However, it could be argued that the main reasons for Islam's growth is not a turn to religious beliefs but due to demographics (e.g. higher fertility rate of Muslims women).

- **Rise in religious fundamentalism.** Evidence shows that, far from secularisation happening in the Middle East, in fact there has been a revival of Islam, especially a rise in fundamentalism in countries such as Syria, Iran, Iraq and Afghanistan, which have reverted back to the creation of Islamic states (accepting the Sharia law). According to Saudi Press Agency, there has also been a significant rise in the number of Muslim taking the haji (the annual pilgrimage to the holy city of Mecca). The number in 1950 was less than 100,00 by 2015, 1.5 million (per annum).

USA (Christianity)
Statistical evidence shows religion remain strong

- America arguably the most rationalistic and technological advance country in the world, should show strong evidence of secularisation occurring, as suggested by Bruce (scientific/technology explanation) Weber (disenchantment explanation). However, Church attendance and membership in America has always been much higher than Western Europe. Americans still consider themselves as very religious. In 1940, 40% of Americans went to church every Sunday. In 2014, the percentage rose to 43%-45%. The proportion saying, they believe in God remained around 95%, which has not changed much since 1944. Some religious groups, particularly Christian conservative fundamentalist groups have increased in number. Religious television programming ('televangalist') has grown considerably, with over 20 million viewers. (Pew Research Centre, 2014). This suggests it is incorrect to argue secularisation is occurring in all modern societies.

Explanations for high levels of religiosity

- **Statistical evidence questionable.** Hadaway et al (1993) has questioned the statistical evidence to show high level of religiosity amongst Americans. He carried out a head count at church services and interviews (that asked how often they attended church) in Ohio. They found that the level of attendance claimed by the participants was 83% higher than what THE researchers estimates of church attendance. This suggest that statistical evidence that show the high levels of religiosity of America, needs to be treated with caution as they may not be reliable or valid. Also the research findings which would support the view that secularisation is occurring.

- **Amercianism.** Herberg (1960) argues that the religious belief systems of churches have now become more secular in order to retain their members (e.g. dilute religious ideas such as creation story). The argument has been applied especially to the major denominations in the USA, which have a high church attendance. Herberg also argues that the reason for high church attendance cannot be found in the congregation's deep religious conviction of faith but that the church now represents the 'American way of life' rather than the word of God. Religion is "something that reassures him about the essential rightness of everything American, his nature, culture and himself." This is supported by Bellah (1976) who argues that the high level of religiosity in the USA is because followers are really expressing through the chuch what it means to be American – "Americanism", rather than religious beliefs. He argues that to be an atheists is 'un-American', so to be religious shows strong patriotism.

- **Cultural defence.** Bruce (1996) put forward the 'cultural defence' argument for as explanation for the high levels of religious beliefs in America. The rapid social change in American in terms of ethnic and racial make-up, social condition and the advancement of technology and modernisation have meant many American have turned to religion. This may explain why there is high levels of church attendance and beliefs amongst Hispanic and African-Americans than general American population, as they cling onto familiar institution (their religion) in an unfamiliar and strange land.

The AQA specification:

- **The significance of religion and religiosity in the contemporary world,** including the nature and extent of secularisation in a global context, and globalisation and the spread of religions

The exam requires that you are able to:

▶ Describe why religion may not be declining, and thus refute secularisation is occurring:

▶ Evaluate the view that secularisation may not be occurring.

The continuing significance of religion in the world

Some critics of secularisation argue that religion is not declining in Western Europe, but rather the way that belief is expressed by people has changed. Others concede that it is occurring mainly in the Western Europe, but not on a global scale. In a changing modern global world, greater individualism, choice and consumerism has also impacted on people's behaviour; new form of religious expression/behaviours has occurred.

Believing without belonging

- According to Grace Davie (2007) the decline of institutional religion does not necessarily mean the decline of religiosity. She argues that religion has become **Privatised.** This means has become a private individual affair. She believes religious beliefs remain strong but people no longer feel it is obligatory to express in religious organisation i.e. churches. The shift from institutionalised to individualised worshipping has meant, according to Davie, we now have people **believing without belonging** – attendance is not necessary.

- Davie also argues that although in Britain attendance is low, there has been a shift towards **vicarious religion**. This means that a minority of people are religious on the behalf of the silent majority i.e. our religious beliefs are expressed by others. For example, a clergymen perform important service such as important memorials, funeral, weddings, baptism and debate controversial moral issues e.g. same-sex marriages. If this not offered, this will call offence to the public. They are there to perform public functions and social roles on behalf of us all. After the sinking of the `Estonia', for instance, the Swedes, supposedly a very secular people, instinctively went to their churches, and the Archbishop knew that it was his role to speak on their behalf. This suggest that 'individualism' may have led people to feeling that their religious believes are private, and a consequence they may not feel the need to make them public by worshipping in private. Davies believing without belonging questions whether secularisation is happening across Europe.

✓✗ Evaluation

> ✗ **Religious beliefs in decline**
>
> The concept 'believing without belonging' has been criticised by empirical evidence. The British social surveys and others consistently show religious beliefs is declining in much at a much faster rate than attendance (Voas, 2013). Also if there is a correlation between decline public worshiping to private worshiping, then according to Davie, the decline of church attendance should see higher levels of beliefs. As the surveys show, this is not the case.

Cultural amensia

Hervieu-Leger (2000) supports Davie's argument for 'believing without belonging' and personal choice. She agrees that there has been a decline in institutional religion in Europe, with fewer people attending church in most countries as people do not feel obliged to attend church services. She says this is because:

- **Cultural amnesia.** the younger generation are experiencing *'cultural amnesia'*. This means the older generation no longer pass on their religious beliefs, values and traditions effectively to the younger generation (through family); fewer parents now teach their children about religion. As a result, the younger generation in today's society have lost the religion that used to be handed down from generation to generation and it has allowed the younger generation to decide which religion to follow themselves.

- **Gender equality.** As there has been a move towards gender equality in society, this has undermined the traditional Church's power to impose patriarchal beliefs on people, Therefore, young people no longer influenced by mainstream organised religions values and beliefs. Also because they see church as being patriarchal, they are more likely to reject traditional churches religious ideology.

- **Spiritual shoppers.** In the modern society, where peoples' beliefs in individual expressionism and in a world of consumer choices this has replaced the accepted of collective traditions and dogmas. Religion is now more individualised as we now develop our own do-it-yourself beliefs that fit our needs and lifestyle, as an alternative to uncritically accepting institutionalised religion. People now feel they have a choice as a consumer of religion, they have become spiritual shoppers; a personal spiritual journey. Hervieu-Leger claims that two religious types are emerging: pilgrims (follow their own path e.g. New Age) and converts (join religious groups with a strong sense of belonging e.g. evangelic churches).

Postmodernists

Postmodernists suggest that religion is in a state of change rather than decline. They argue that there is a demand for spirituality motivated by increasing *individuation* that cannot be catered for by any one religion.

Lyon: Jesus in Disneyland

Lyon (2000) a postmodernist, suggests with the impact of globalisation, especially the accessibility of information, and the increased importance of the media and consumerism and the desire for greater individualism in people, has meant the nature of religious behaviour has changed. This has given rise to new forms of religion, which still demonstrates a strong religiosity in society. According to Lyon, religion has changed by:

- **Religion as a consumer product.** Lyon, a postmodernist, in his 'Jesus in Disneyland' book, shows how Christianity has changed itself into a new form for the modern consumer. He gives an example of the Harvest Day Crusade held in Disneyland California, attended by over 10,000 Christians in which several artists and a preacher performed on stage. This Evangelical organisation strategically placed itself in Disney theme park suggests in order to market themselves within a popular culture to appeal to as many consumers as possible –to present 'their faith' as an attraction for our consumption.

- **The relocation of religion.** there has been a relocation of religion, where religious ideas have been 'disembedded' as the media lift them out of their original local contexts, and move them to a different time and place e.g. televangelism and the electronic church can be accessed from home. This means religion has been de-institutionalised, as it allows people to express their beliefs without actually going to church, and this support Davies 'believing without belonging'.

- **Spiritual shopping.** In a postmodern world, our person identities are now constructed by what we consume, including religious beliefs, from a global market place. According to Lyon, people have become 'spiritual shoppers'. The choice of an assortment of beliefs and practices over the internet has given rise to a 'spiritual supermarket' in which individuals can construct their belief systems around a 'pick and mix' approach to religion. Selecting aspect of religious ideas that best suits them. This shows that people may cease to belong to a traditional mainstream religious organisation, instead they've become 'religious consumers' construing their own religious beliefs. For example, Madonna is a 'spiritual shopper', 'religious consumer' and fits in with the notion of pick and mix, as she follows a range of beliefs stemming from Catholicism, Kabbalah (Judaism) and yoga (Buddhism).

- He argues that religion is going through a process of Disneyfication – a process of mass marketing that uses a range of global media including film, television, music websites and social networking platforms to sell its 'religion'.

✓✗ Evaluation

> ✗ **Empirical evidence for consumerism**
> There is empirical evidence to support Lyon's religious as a form of consumerism by the increasing growth of 'televangelism' and 'Islamic televangelism'. However, Lyon's religious consumerism has been criticised. Bruce (2002) argues that Lyon's notion of 'consumerist religion' present a weak type of religion; he argues that consumption is increasingly *replacing* religion, in terms of providing people with meaning in their lives, rather than facilitating its continuation. He argues that the rise is in consumerist religions is evidence for secularisation and not the continuing emergence and renewal of religiosity.

Religious market theory

Those who support the view that secularisation is occurring point towards that the growing trend of religious diversity (pluralism); the array of different and competing religious institutions. Stark and Bainbridge's (1985) religious market theory (or know as rational choice theory) argue against this. The theory is bases in two assumptions:

- **Religion as a compensator.** They suggest that there will be a constant demand for religion, because it provides us with *compensators*. People seek rewards (e.g. material wealth) that can be unobtainable, so they compensate for this. They turn to religious compensators rather than secular compensators because they can invoke God and make promises about the next world (e.g. supernatural rewards, e.g. promises of an afterlife). Since the desire for rewards always outstrips their availability, the demand for religion will be a constant, and thus the decline of religion) is unlikely to occur.

- **Religion as a competitive business.** Religious organisations are now like business that compete in the spiritual marketplace for customers. People make rational choices based on the cost-benefits analysis of the available religious options, when they buy or consume religion (*cost* = financial, investment in time; *benefit*=spiritual fulfilment, more friends). Diversity, choice and competition between religious organisations leads to greater variety of religion and improved quality of religious product, constantly adapted and tailored to the need of the consumer, which lead to more religious participation; the churches that make their products attractive will attract the most 'customers', those that don't, will decline.

- **The cycle of religious renewal.** Stark and Bainbridge point to historical evidence to show that religion goes through a cycle of decline, revival and renewal. There is a perceptual cycle of how religion behaves in society;

with some declining and others growing and attracting new members. They argue that religious pluralism/ diversity is evidence of the high levels of religiosity that continues to exit in people.

- **America v Europe.** Stark and Finke (2000) argues that demand for religion increases when there are different sorts to choose from. When there is not, this can lead to the decline of religion. They make the comparison with Europe and America. In European societies, one main religion dominates, often the official state church e.g. Church of England. Here there is no competition, only one main church which can lead to decline. The lack of suppliers and choice means that only a fraction of people beliefs can be catered for, and thus dampens down religious participants. Therefore, it is the lack of supply of religion rather than secularisation that is leading to decline religion in Europe. In comparison to the USA, church attendance/beliefs is high in America because of the 'supply'; the great variety of religious denominations to choose from. This has resulted in a highly competitive religious market for customers, which would lead to improved services that the churches offer and in turn greater religiosity. They argue that is why religion is still prominent in America.

✓✗ Evaluation

> **✗ Diversity does not promote religiosity**
> The religious market theory has been criticised, as there is statistical evidence that does not support the theory. Firstly, Bruce (2002) argues that there is evidence of secularisation happening both in Europe and America, so religious diversity is not actually promoting religiosity. Bruce also points out that even in United States, there are large areas like the southern states, that do not have a wide diversity of religious denominations, yet participants still remains high.

> **✗ High religiosity where only one church dominates**
> Norris and Inglehart (2011) argue that Stark and Bainbridge's religious market theory fails to explain high religious participation exists in countries where the church has a monopoly and very limited religious diversity (Ireland, and in orthodox Christian Churches e.g. Greece, Cyprus and Serbia), or countries that there is religious pluralism but have now levels of participation (Austria and Netherlands).

Existential security theory

- **Existential security theory.** Norris and Inglehart (2011) criticise the religious market theory because it only applies to America and fails to explain the variations religiosity between different countries. They put forward an *existential security theory* to explain the various levels if religiosity between different countries. The theory argues that if people feel insecure about their 'existence' and future existence and that of their children they may turn to religion for comfort and security. If they feel secure about their life and their family (e.g. high standard of living), there is less need for religious comfort, they take survival for granted.

- **Poor and rich societies.** We can apply the existential theory to explain why religiosity is high (and thus secularisation is low) in developing or poor societies such as Chad, Rwanda and Mali which may face life threating risk such as famine, poverty, disease and war on a daily basis. In comparison to developed and rich countries that enjoys a high levels of existential security, such as Sweden, Norway and Britain, the importance of religions is minimal which may explain why religiosity and church attendance is low.

✓✗ Evaluation

> ✗ **America's high religiosity a challenge to theory**
>
> The existential theory fails to explain the high levels of religiosity and church attendance in the United States—the world's richest country, where people have a high level if existential security. However, Norris and Inglehart argue that high levels of religiosity in American is because they still feel the risk of 'insecurity to their existence. The stark social class inequality of US society, combined with inadequate social welfare and healthcare system, create high levels of poverty and insecurity for the poorest groups, which helps to explain higher levels of religiosity. This insecurity may also apply to the non-poor, who may face for example, the threat of huge crippling medical bills if they fall ill.

> ✗ **Enlightenment the real reason?**
>
> Some sociologists have criticised this theory because they argue that it is not the low levels if wealth and lifestyle of a society that is responsible for secularisation but rather education, as this encourages people to become more rational and enlighten in their thinking. Furthermore, Norris and Inglehart see religion as a negative response to deprivation/poverty but ignore the positive reasons, such as why religion appeals to the wealthy.

Conclusion

- The continuation of religious beliefs, especially globally, has meant that secularisation proves difficult to determine. There are regional variations. Statistical evidence suggests that some northern western societies are becoming secular, where others southern European are not experiences the process of secularism. The revival of religious fever in some parts of the world (especially in the Middle East and the USA) suggests that, far from secularisation occurring, there has been a revival of religiosity. As Giddens (2001) argues, religion is becoming more important in the modern world.

Exam Questions

1. Outline and explain **two** causes for the process of secularisation.. . . . .[10 marks]

2. Outline and explain two ways in which the growth of sects and New Age movements may be related to secularisation.. . . . .[10 marks]

3. Outline and explain **two** reasons why attendance in church might be in decline.. . . . .[10 marks]

4. Applying material from **Item...** analyse **two** reasons why high church attendance tell us very little about the level of religiosity in a society. . . . .[10 marks]

5. Applying material from **Item...** and your knowledge, evaluate the claim that religion in modem society, religious beliefs and religious behaviour are changing rather than declining. . .[20 marks]

6. Applying material from **Item...** and your knowledge, evaluate the extent of secularisation in society today. . . . .[20 marks]

7. Applying material from **Item...** and your knowledge, evaluate the view that while church attendance in England is declining, other religions and spiritual movements are flourishing. . .[20 marks]

8. Applying material from **Item...** and your knowledge, evaluate the view that religion is now about consumerism, where spiritual shoppers look in the spiritual marketplace for a product that suits their lifestyle.. . . . .[20 marks]

The AQA specification:

- The significance of religion and religiosity in the contemporary world, including the nature and extent of secularisation in a global context, and globalisation and the spread of religions

The exam requires that you are able to:

▶ Describe the effect globalisation has had on religion.
▶ Evaluate the effect globalisation has had on religion.

Globalisation and the spread of religion

Globalization can be defined as the increasing flow of people, information, culture, services, and other resources across national boundaries as a process of an ever growing interconnectedness of the countries and societies around the world.

- **More tolerant of other faiths.** The impact of globalization on religion has meant the growth of religious diversity, which means we are now in closer contract with people of other faith than ever before; not just locally but globally via internet and social media sites. This has given us a better insight and understanding of what may have been seen as 'alien' religions prior to globalization. Some would argue that, this has led to lessening of intolerance and prejudices to other religions; people are more observance and tolerance of other belief systems, such as the Indian festival Diwali and Ramadan and more signs of Islamic dress code (veiling of women e.g. hijab).

- **Conflict-resolution in times of crisis.** Bandchoff (2008) argues that globalization has promoted greater interreligious dialogue in political and social world affairs than ever before. This has led religious leaders drawn from the world's leading religious traditions—Christian, Muslim, Jewish, etc. to endorsed common values such as peace and tolerance. For example, the terrorist attacks in Paris in 201 led Muslim leaders around the world to condemn such acts in the name of Islam. Globalization allows for religions previously isolated from one another to now have regular contact and can be used as conflict resolution in times of crisis.

- **Deterriorialization.** The impact of globalisation has led to the *deterriorialization* of religion. This means religious beliefs and practices are less tied to particular geographical locations, culture and population group. This consequence of this, is that religious beliefs and organisation will eventually be assimilated across the globe and religion will become **transnational**— without defined territorial boundaries. Individuals will be able to 'mix' and 'match' elements of religious beliefs system that appeals to them. This means can undermine the authority and control of traditional religious organisation as beliefs becomes diluted.

- **Clash of civilisation and culture wars.** According to Huntington (1990), argues that the consequences of globalisation has paved the way for cultures and religions to come in direct contacts with one another which will lead to conflicts to occur between the world's major civilizations—clash of civilisation, such as the Western Christianity and Islam. For example, the growth of Islam increasing comes into conflict with Christian based Western civilisation. Such as the war in Afghanistan, 9/11 attacks on the World Trade Centre in New York in 2011, or the London bombing on 7th of July 2005.

- Inglenhart and Norris (2011) argues that Huntington's clash of civilization thesis is partly true but it is not just the Muslim world rejection of democracy, it also mainly due to the **sexual clash of civilizations** – how Muslim countries treat women. Inglenhart and Norris (2011) analyse data from the World Values Survey and found that the support for democracy is similarly high in both West and the Muslim world, but there are great differences when it comes to gender equality and sexual liberalization e.g. divorce, marriage, dating, abortion, and gay rights. This suggest that the West is more liberal and the Muslim's more traditional values, is the real class of civilisation.

- **Fundamentalism.** Globalisation has also meant the spread of western culture, in particularly American culture in the Islamic world. According to Bruce (2002), the impact of globalization has given rise to religious Islamic fundamentalist as means of cultural defence, to 'defend' and attempt to restore traditional fundamental cultural and religious values from western imperialism and western secular values in Islamic cultures. As a consequence, such fundamentalist groups may adopt an aggressive approach to their perceived threat to their existence e.g. the attack on the World Trade Centre (9/11), the terrorist attacks by ISIS in Paris, 2015 and the growth of the Islamic State in Iraq and Syria" (ISIS). Similarly, Giddens (1999) see fundamentalist as a response to the globalisation of western cultures and lifestyle. For example, Islamic fundamentalist groups (e.g. Taliban, ISIS) see their way of life being eroded by liberal influences from the west such as equality for women, gay rights, sexual liberalisation of women-marriage, divorce and dating etc.).

- Globalisation, primarily due to the technological innovations of the information age has meant that the modern fundamentalist terrorist religious groups have become transnational; they are now global and decentralized, unlike the past. Recruiting new followers to their ideology and beliefs are no longer restricted by geographical boundaries; but can be recruited worldwide. For example, the religious groups ISIS, ideological brainwashing often takes place on the Internet (forums/chat rooms). Acts of terror, that require technical knowledge needed or suicide attacks are learned are now conducted via online. In principle, anyone can act on behalf of religious group such known as the 'lone wolf'. A lone wolf (lone-wolf terrorist) is someone who prepares and commits violent acts alone, without having assistance from the group— they have acted independently. They may be influenced or motivated by the ideology and beliefs, and may act in support of such a group.

✓✗ Evaluation

✗ Globalisation has led to less tolerance and freedom
The view that the effects of globalization on religion has brought greater tolerance has been challenged. Ben-Nun Bloom et al (2014) suggest that globalisation has contributed to the decline of religious freedom across the world. More countries are interfering with worship and other religious practices such as regulating religious symbols, literature and broadcasting. For example, the 'burqa ban' in several European counties such as France. Globalisation of religion has meant, that native countries preserve their existing traditional and values from different religions belief and customs.

✗ Supporting evidence for deterriorialization of religion
There is supporting empirical evidence that the impact of globalisation has led to the deterriorialization of religion. Singleton (2014) cites Islam as an example of a religion becoming transnational. There is a growing emphasis Islamic 'ummah' –refers to a worldwide community faith with shared beliefs and practices, that transcends national borders, cultures or ethnicity. For example, the publication in 2005 of the prophet Mohammed in Danish Newspaper, was regarded as insult, which led to a worldwide protest by the Muslim community, despite their cultural and social differences.

✗ Ignores conflict within the same civilisation
Casanova (2005) criticises of Huntington's clash of civilisation view because he ignores the many conflicts and clashes within the same civilisations, such as the conflict between the two different forms of Islam; the Sunni and Shia, (Iran-Iraq war). Horrie and Chippindale (2007) argues that his 'clash of civilisation' is misleading because it is the neo-conservative ideology (from the western world) that portrays Islam as the enemy. In reality only a minority are interested in a holy war against the west. Karen Armstrong (2015) suggest that hostility from the West does not stem from fundamentalist Islam but a reaction to Western foreign policy in the Middle East e.g. the Western world supporting Israel-Palestine conflict.

Exam Questions

1. Outline and explain **two** ways in which religion and development may be related in the world today . . . .[10 marks]

2. Applying material from **Item...** and your knowledge, evaluate the view that growth of religious fundamentalism is a reaction to globalisation. . . . .[20 marks]

The AQA specification:

- The religious organisations, including cults, sects, denominations, churches and New Age movements, and their relationship to religious and spiritual belief and practice

The exam requires that you are able to:

▶ Describe and evaluate the characteristics of the different types of religious/spiritual organisations.
▶ Explain and evaluate the reasons for the growth or decline of religious/spiritual organisations.

The main types of religious organisations

There are different religious organisations, but there is a great deal of variation between them in terms of commitment required, their relationship they have with outside world, and how they are organised and so on. Sociologists are interested in the different types of religious organisations that have flourished and have attempted to create a **typology**; classifying them into according to typical characteristics. They are also interested why people join them and why some are short-lived and others are not. Broadly speaking, there are four main forms of religious organisations that have been identified:

- Church
- Denominations
- Sects
- Cults

Types of Religious Organisations

Churches and Sects

Weber (1920) made the original distinction between two different types of religious organisations – **churches** and **sects** within Christianity. However, it was his friend Ernst Troeltsch (1931) who developed these distinctions further. Sects can be seen as a small religion that has broken away from the official established mainstream church of society, often due to the differences in the interpretation of religious teachings. Although the definition of 'church' by Weber and Troeltsch was originally based on Western Christian organisations, it can still be applicable to other faiths and in other countries that shares similar characteristics of a 'church'.

Churches

Summary of a church: The term 'church' is applied in societies were a single religion organisation really dominates society, which is predominately the main faith of the population. Often seen as the 'official religion' of the state which legal privileges and can often influence the state on social, political and educational matters. Churches are a well-established religious organisation, that has a formal hierarchal, bureaucratic and organised structure.

Examples	• *Christianity:* Church of England (England); Roman Catholics Church (Italy, Spain); Orthodox Church (Greece, Cyprus).
Structure	• A large organisation that has a formal hierarchal and bureaucratic with paid official (e.g. in the Catholic religion the Pope heads a pyramid of cardinals, archbishops, bishops and priests).
Size	• Size of church membership tends to be the very large, the largest religious organisational type e.g. millions of people.

Membership	• Membership is inclusive, means it's open to all types of people and are from all social backgrounds. Members are predominately born into the church or self-recruited by conversion. • Churches tend to have a particularly link to the socially powerful people/upper classes. For instance, the queen and the Church of England.
Commitment	• Makes few demands on members – possible to be a member without ever attending collective worship (becoming a member, usually mean no drastic life change). However, the church encourages regular attendance and involvement.
View of society	• Accepts the main values and norms of society. Often seen as the 'official religion' of the state—country (e.g. Queen being the head of the state and the Church of England). Often integrated into the social, moral and economic structure of society.
View of other beliefs/ religions	• Believes it has a monopoly on truth (their teachings are the only one being true and the only legitimate religion). They do not accept other religions as being true. • Its beliefs and values are accepted by the majority of the population.

Sects

Summary of a sect Sects tend to be much smaller and in conflict (even hostile) with the values and normal of society – often rejecting the teachings of the church, and hence, leads them to break away from the main church, and thus are become a 'sect' from the main religion.

Examples	• Christianity: Jehovah witnesses, Unification Church (the Moonies); Amish.; Peoples Temple, Branch Davidians, Quakers
Structure	• Often no hierarchal structure or paid officials; but more egalitarian in structure, often under the control of a single influential charismatic leader.
Size	• Size of membership tends to be small • Life span of sects can be short lived (possibly until the leader dies).
Membership	• Membership is exclusive – tight entry criteria, possibly through recommendation. Often requires very strong commitment from its members. See themselves as an 'exclusive group' – which usually requires a change or to withdraw from current lifestyle.
Commitment	• High level of commitment required. People that join tend to be lower working class (the poor); the oppressed and marginalised.
View of society	• They often reject society and the state; often in conflict/hostile or disapproving of society's' values and norms and aim to replace them with alternative beliefs and practises. • Can be anti-establishment and anti-authority, therefore often viewed as a deviant religious organisation.
View of other beliefs/ religions	• May makes absolute truth claims on religious beliefs (monopoly over truth claims); not accepting of other religions/beliefs.

Denominations

As sects became established in society and the membership, grows in size, it was difficult to categorise them as either a church-types or sect-type organisation. As a result of this, Richard Niebuhr (1929) introduced a distinct religious organisation called *denominations* which can be viewed as a halfway between a church and a sect.

Summary of a denomination: An established religious organisation that has a hierarchal and organised structure, much bigger in size of membership than a sect, although the size of members and structure is smaller than a church. Denominations are tolerant and accepting of the values of society, although they have no influence on the state or the majority of the population.

Examples	• *Christianity:* Baptist Church, Methodist Church, Pentecostal Church.
Structure	• Quite a large organisation that has a formal hierarchal and bureaucratic structure with paid official, although there often have unpaid or lay preachers as well.
Size	• Size of membership tends to be large.
Membership	• Membership is inclusive means it's open to all types of people or through family tradition. Denominations often have members from working-class and lower middle-class backgrounds.

New Religious Movements (NRMs)

Since the 1960s there has been a rapid growth of cults and sects, this made it difficult to classify them under one particular type. This led Roy Wallis (1984) to reject the typology outlined by Troeltsch for a number of reasons: firstly, sect and cult are negatively loaded as terms and imply some judgement of the organisations, secondly some religious organisations didn't fit neatly into the previous categories. For example, the Hindu-based Siddha Yoga movement one cannot be sure if this is a cult or a sect. So instead of referring to them as 'denominations', 'sects' or 'cults', Wallis (1984) coined the term New Religious Movements. This is a broader updated classification system/typology in which he divides them into three main groups based on their relationship to the outside world.

1. **World-accommodating.** *Similar characteristics as a denomination.* They are often offshoots of churches. These religious organisations are critical or dissatisfied with some aspects of wider society as well as mainstream religions and often seek to revert back to the pure religious teachings of their faith – conservative beliefs (e.g. against divorce, abortion, contraception, anti-abortion, anti-gay rights). Individuals feel that they can redress this situation in their own lives without cutting themselves off from the wider society.
Examples: Baptist churches, Methodist Churches, Pentecostal Churches.

2. **World-affirming groups.** *Similar characteristics as a cult.* These types of religious organisation are less religious and focus more on human development, such as self-improvement therapies and psychologies attempting to develop and release 'human potential and growth' enabling participants to become more successful members of society. They do not require a major change from conventional lifestyle.
Examples: Church of Scientology, Human Potential Movement, Transcendental Meditation.

3. **World-rejecting groups.** *Similar characteristics to a sect.* They often very hostile, critical or rejecting of mainstream society. Membership is often based on exclusive entry, often led by an influential charismatic leader, a high level of commitment is required and demands its members to sacrifice a great deal to be part of the organisation; which may entail a sharp break with conventional life and significant lifestyle changes.
Examples: The International Society for Krishna Consciousness (ISKCON-Hare Krishna), Branch Davidians, Peoples' Temple and ISIS

Stark and Bainbridge (1985) are critical of the previous typologies of religious organisations as they claimed the criteria was too broad, which mean there were many similar characteristics that tend to be found in each group, resulting in confusion and contradictions, and thus should be abandoned. Instead they argue for a much tighter basic criterion, were religious groups can be compared in terms of a single criterion: the degree of conflict that exists between them and the wider society. Such a definition allows clear comparisons and changes over time to be described. They suggest that:

- Sects are an offshoot of an existing religion as a result of schism (split) due to difference in interpretation or religious doctrine/practises.

- Cults can be defined in terms as new religion in society or one that is new to that particular society (e.g. Scientology in the UK). There are three types of cults according to their degrees of organisation:

   o *Audience cult:* the least formal and organised cult, with no membership, with little interaction, but may hold occasional meetings. For example, astrology believers share the common belief but do not necessarily know each other as they don't have massive gatherings.

- Client cults: a more formal and organised cult, usually offer services to the followers – client/practitioner relationship. For example, Scientology offers to clear 'engrams' (e.g. repressed memories of painful experiences) for followers.

- Cult movements: the most formal and organised cult, that demands a high level of commitment than other cults. Many client cults can develop into cult movements for their most dedicated followers, e.g. members of Heaven's Gate cult committed suicide when a comet crossed the sky in 1997, holding the belief that such act would bring them to heaven.

✓✗ Evaluation

✓ **The strengths of Wallis new topology.**

Wallis does not argue that all religious group will fall exactly into one of his three categories. Consequently, he acknowledges that some groups fall in the 'middle ground' between two or more of his types. Furthermore, his topology avoids some of the stigma associated with grouping some religions as sect or a cult.

✗ **New classification necessary?**

A criticism of classifying the different religions under Wallis's newer typology, is that it does not really help in creating a better understanding of the existing classification of religious organisations (e.g. denominations, sects and cults). Hadden (2003) argues that the definition of world-rejecting NRMs is so close to that of sects that it makes no difference which term is used.

✗ **Problem of classification**

Some NRMs cannot be categorised under Wallis's classification system. For example, the Unification Church (Moonies) cannot be classified in the existing type because it incorporates religious ideas from a variety of sources such as Christianity, Taoism, Confucianism and elements of other modern ideas. So it makes it difficult to determine the type of relationship this organisation has to the outside world—world accommodating; world-rejecting or world-affirming?

✗ **Eurocentric**

Wallis NRMs typology is based within a Christian and European tradition, which makes it difficult to be applied to non-Christian religions. Therefore, it is only applicable to European countries.

✗ **Methodological issues**

Some NRMs are extremely difficult to investigate, especially those that are more deviant and secretive, where accessibility will be almost impossible. Therefore, at times knowledge will be based on secondary data which makes this difficult to classify under a particular category.

✗ **Differences within a religious organisation**

It is wrong to assume that the views of members are homogeneous (being all the same for all) there may be a range of views and outlook within a particular NRM, which can influence how they perceive and interact with the outside world, with some being accommodating while other may take a harder stance and be rejecting. This means individual difference may influence what typology the NRM potentially could fall under.

Reasons for the Growth of NRMs

Sociologists offer several explanations for their rapid growth and appeal of newreligious movements (sects and cults) the 1960s:

Marginality

- Max Weber (1963) offers one of the earliest explanation for the growth of sects. He argues that sects appeal to the social groups whom feel they are marginalised and disadvantaged in society; usually the working class and lower-middle class. This is because sects provide a solution for those who see themselves lacking in 'social' and 'status' recognition in society, by offering what Weber calls **theodicy of disprivilege:** a religious explanation for their disadvantage, by offering of better life in the afterlife or in future society after divine intervention.

- Max Weber (1963) offers one of the earliest explanation for the growth of sects. He argues that sects appeal to the social groups whom feel they are marginalised and disadvantaged in society; usually the working class and lower-middle class. This is because sects provide a solution for those who see themselves lacking in 'social' and 'status' recognition in society, by offering what Weber calls theodicy of disprivilege: a religious explanation for their disadvantage, by offering of better life in the afterlife or in future society after divine intervention.

- Bellah gives the example of the continuing marginalisation of Black Americans since WW2 has led many to seek refuge in NRMs, especially Black Muslims. The growth of the sect called *Nation of Islam* can be seen as a response to the increasing hardship of the ghetto (e.g. poverty, bad housing, unemployment). In the Black Muslim movement – which grew especially in the 1960s – individuals found friendship and emotional support. Members were encouraged to believe that Blacks were by nature "divine" and were superior to Whites. On initiation, Blacks replaced their slave name with Muslim name and transformed their negative identity to a positive one. Believers were required to follow a strict moral code (e.g. no alcohol) and encouraged to look after each other's welfare. Their ultimate goal was Black supremacy.

Relative deprivation

- The marginality fails to explain the popularity of NRMs amongst white, middle class males. Many NRMs e.g. The Christian Science Movement, have a largely middle class membership. It is possible that some individual who are affluent (e.g. income, housing) may feel themselves to be 'deprived' or 'disadvantaged' by comparing themselves to others, especially their reference groups such as friends, siblings and so on. If this is the case, they have experienced feelings of *relative deprivation*. So whilst they have don't lack material wealth, they may feel **spiritually deprived.** In fact, material success can heighten these feelings. Hence, they have joined NRMs to find peace of mind & spiritual fulfilment.

Social change

- Wilson (1982) argues that the appeal of world religious movements is often occurs at a time of rapid social change or disruption in society; which undermine or threaten the norms of society. This can result in a producing a feeling of social dislocation and **anomie** (normlessness) where guidelines of social behaviour are no longer in place. Wilson argues that a number of circumstances can produce these feelings such as war, economic collapse and natural disaster. For some the rapid social change will seem attractive. They offer certainty, warmth and the support of a community which gives its members a reason for living. Two explanations are given for both world rejecting NRM and world affirming NRM:

- *World rejecting NRM.* The 1960s and 1970s saw a rapid increase in urbanisation and industrialisation in western countries. This led to the breakdown in community and the feelings of anonymity. People sought refuge in religious groups like Hare Krishna; particularly amongst the young and affluent. In these, members are able to find security or friendship, as well as strong systems of faith.

- *World affirming NRM.* Bruce (1995) suggest that the growth of world affirming movements have been a response to modernisation, especially the rationalisation of work. This is because people find it increasingly difficult to gain satisfaction and sense of identity from work. These groups offer people both success and a spiritual element to their lives.

✓✗ Evaluation

> **✗ Research evidence against 'marginality' explanation**
>
> There is research evidence that does not support the view that those from disadvantaged groups tend to join sects. Eileen Barker (1984) found that while studying the religious group, the 'Moonies' most members of NRMs come from happy, middle class homes. This suggests that membership of NRMs is not only confined to the lower levels of society. However, Wallis argues that this doesn't contradict the marginality theory as many of the recruits had become marginal because they were "hippies, drop-outs, surfers LSD and marijuana users".

> **✗ Research evidence against 'social change' explanation**
>
> There is research evidence that does not support the view that social change leads to people joining sects. Stark and Bainbridge (1985) analysed the percentages in the USA in different time periods during the first three quarters of the 20th century. They found 16% were formed in the 1950s, a period of stability,14% in the 1960s and only 3% from 1970-1977. The 1960s and 1970s were a time of social unrest with student demonstrations, hippie movement, black riots and the Vietnam war. This seems to question the view that sects develop during periods of social change. However, Stark and Bainbridge used a limied definition of a sect – a breakaway from established religion. A broader definition may result in a different figures and a different conclusion.

The dynamic of sects/NRMs

Studies have shown that some sects and NRMs, once established, eventually turn into a denomination, while others have shown that many are short-lived and eventually die out. A number of sociologists have put forward explanations for this.

Reasons why sects are short-lived

Neibuhr (1929) study of sects in America found that sects either will die out within one generation, or they must reconcile with society, by 'cooling down' their extreme views and become a denomination. Neibuhr puts several reasons why sects/NRM are short-lived:

- *Second generation lacks the commitment.* The original generation of sect members join by making a substantial commitment to the organisation. Many new members and children of these original members rarely have the same degree of religious zest and commitment to the organisation, and thus many drop out over time.

- *Death/loss of charismatic leaders.* Sects/NRMs tend to be founded by a single charismatic leader. If the leader dies, then it likely that sect will also die and any subsequent leaders rarely have the same authority and personal characteristics. For example, the Branch Davidians had a highly charismatic leader called David Koresh, that once he died the organisation also perished. This begins the process of the organisation evolving the bureaucratic hierarchy of more denomination-like organisation – transforming the sect into a denomination.

- *Reasons for joining no longer present.* Some of the reasons why an individual initially joined may no longer be present Many members experience social mobility and with this the feeling of social integration that they lacked previously (and which led them to join the sect). This success can mean that believers have no further need for the sect – causing it to die out.

- *Too extreme.* Some sects/NRMs are so marginalised from wider society it is very difficult for them to continue to survive as they are unlikely to recruit new members with such extreme beliefs or practices. Alternatively, the sect could continue in a less radical fashion – becoming less hostile to the wider society (which members are now integrated into) and more denomination-like (e.g. Methodism).

Sects/NRMs are not always short-lived

Wilson (1959) argues that not all sects disappear over time or that some turn into denominations; that is not the only choice they have. Some sects continue to survive and remain as a sect. For instance, Jehovah's Witness and Seventh Day Adventist are example of established long standing Christian sects. According to Wilson for a sect to retain its sect status or become a denomination, depends on how the sect offers its members to be 'saved' (i.e. salvation).

- *Conversionist sects* are the most likely to develop into denominations. These believe that the only way to salvation into heaven is to be born again which requires individuals to 'convert'. Their aim is to convert as many people as possible to God through evangelical preaching. To do this on a wide scale, they eventually have to: [1] evolve a bureaucratic structure and a paid hierarchy of officials; [2] They must also maintain constant contact with the outside world (from which new converts are, of course, drawn). If such sects are successful in recruiting a large number of individuals this can turn into a denomination e.g. The Salvation Army that has turned from a conversionist sect into a denomination.

- *Adventist sects (revolutionary sect)* tend to believe in a 'doomsday' scenario that a divine intervention or imminent radical transformation in the world will occur (e.g. Second coming of Christ) where evil will be defeated. In order to be 'saved', members are required to remove themselves from the corrupt world. This separatist approach can prevent sects from becoming a denomination. E.g. Jehovah witness.

- *Introversionist sects* believe in not compromising their religious conviction to God; a compromise in their religious practise may not guarantee them salvation. In order to be 'saved', they have to cut themselves completely from the outside world and remain as a marginalised community (e.g. Amish and Mormons). Such disengaged sects often remain as they are and very unlikely to change into a denomination.

New Age Movements (NAMs)

Since the 1980's a new type of unconventional religious organisation has emerged called **new age movements**. Although they have very similar characteristics as cults, Heelas (1996) suggests that NAMs are primarily concerned with mind-body ideas: the achievement of self-discovery, personal growth, self-perfection, the harnessing of inner potential and spiritual awareness, and often involve a rejection of scientific and rational logic. The beliefs and practices, are often derived from environmentalism, alternative medicine and therapies, eastern and western philosophies and psychology. For example, crystal therapy, clairvoyance, psychic healing, feng shui, astrology, tarot, reincarnation, Wicca (witchcraft), shamanism and palmistry. According to Bruce (2002), some of the main common themes of NAMs and what that separate them from mainstream religions are:

- *A belief in the notion of inner human potential* – new age ideas aim to connect you with your inner-self to maximize your potential to make you happier, healthier and more successful.

- *Therapeutic techniques* – new age ideas tend to be therapeutic. Followers of new age believe this can be unlocked by new age therapeutic techniques in order to improve themselves (as above).

- *A belief in natural energy* – the idea that good and bad energy exist, which can have an impact on human behaviour. Some NAM prove techniques to control negative energy e.g. crystals, aromas and feng shui, wearing metal bangles etc.

- *Everything is connected* – NAMs take a holistic approach. They see the 'Self' (mind, body and spirit) being connected and influenced from the environment, the supernatural and cosmos, as we are all part of the greater whole.

✓✗ Evaluation

> **✗ Difference between a NAM and a cult?**
> A criticism of classifying some religions as 'new age movements' is that it is difficult to distinguish a NAM from a cult (or world-affirming). This raises the question why create another religious category, when you can group them under the classification as 'cults'. Adding an additional classification creates more confusion to an already confusing classification system.

> **✗ NAM are not a religion**
> A further criticism of classifying NAM as a type of religious organisation, is that some sociologists have argued that many NAM are essentially not a religion. Many do not have collective worshipping, beliefs or supernatural power element to them. For example, Shiatsu message, herbalism, mindfulness and yoga have no religious characteristics, and therefore should not be classified as one.

Reasons for the growth of the new age movement

Some sociologist such as Bruce (1995) see the growth of new age movements as a reflection of modernity rather than postmodernity – a phase rather than a new era/type of society. While other, see new age movement as an expression of postmodernity – a new era which is distinct from modernity. Several explanations for the growth of new age ideas in modernity/postmodernity world:

- **Provides meaning.** According to Bauman (1982) in a postmodernist society, where there has been a growing rejection of grand narratives such as religion and science – people have lost faith in traditional sources of authority which has left has left people with a void in their lives a *crisis of meaning*, to their existence. Postmodernists believe that the growths of NAMs (as well as NRMs) offer individuals meaning and explanations for their existence.

- **Provides spiritual fulfilment and identity.** Heelas (1998) see the growth of New Age ideas as a result of living in a postmodern world. Some of the reasons are for the growth of age movements are:
  - *Consumerism:* a world over-saturated by consumerism has left people feeling dissatisfied with their lives; a lack of spirituality. The new Age offers way to achieve spiritual fulfilment in consumer culture world.
  - *Identity crisis:* the decline of religious traditions, dogmas and the assimilation of cultures, class, ethnicity etc., in a fast changing world, has left people with a fragmented identity; unsure of themselves. New Age beliefs offers a source of identity.

Exam Questions

1. Outline and explain **two** reasons why growth of New Age movements may be a response to conditions of rapid social change . . . .**[10 marks]**

2. Applying material from **Item...** analyse **two** reasons why membership of sects may be short-lived. .**[10 marks]**

3. Applying material from **Item...** and your knowledge, evaluate sociological explanations for the growth of cults, sects and new religious movements. . . . .**[20 marks]**

4. Applying material from **Item...** and your knowledge, evaluate view that cults, sects and New Age movements are fringe organisations which are inevitably short-lived and of little influence in contemporary society . . . .**[20 marks]**

✓✗ Evaluation

✗ Biological role questioned

The evidence linking religion to the biology or women's natural role has been criticised by feminists. This is because they argue that there is no research evidence to show that biological make up of men and women that explain gender differences in religious level. Feminist would argue that more religious nature of women is because their 'expressive role' has been socially constructed by a male in a patriarchal society.

✗ Not gender differences

Some sociologist argue that women are not as in paid employment as men (less likely to working) and for this reason, they have more time on their hand than men to attend religious activities, and thus that is why they are more likely to seem more religious where they may really not be (Miller and Hoffman, 1995).

✗ Age rather than gender differences

The over-representation of women may also have to do with age rather than gender differences. There are more women who attend religious services then men, because a number of church goers are elderly, and there are more elderly women than men because women live longer than men. Furthermore, widowed women may turn to such mainstream religious organisation not for religious reasons but as means of social networking—connecting with other people and making friends.

✗ Concept of God questioned

Feminist would claim that women are not inherently more religious. They argue that if we analyse religious text, masculinity traits such as vengeance, violence and aggression are also regarded as religious qualities as the feminine traits such as compassions are. Feminist therefore would claim that the feminine characteristics of religiosity may simply reflect patriarchal bias.

✗ Women and New Age Moments

Trzebiatowska and Bruce (2012) argues that women tend to associated themselves with new age movements (NAM) for non-religious reason such as health, fitness rather than religious or spiritual growth. This means we must question how we define new age movements, Presently the definition is too broad as it does not differentiate those attend for religious/spiritual and those that do not fall in that category. This means the reasons why women join NAMs may not be completely valid.

✗ Risk theory questioned

The view of the risk theory, that men are more willing to take risks than women, is the reason why men are less religious has been criticised. People who do not believe in God or the afterlife will not be anxious what happened after death. Therefore, they are very unlikely to view their lack of religious beliefs to be down to risk taking behaviour.

Ethnicity and religiosity

The large number of different ethnic minority groups living in the UK, has brought about religious diversity in society. Some of the main ethnic groups in the UK are Afro-Caribbean (Christian), Polish (Christians) Pakistani (Muslim), India (Hindu and Sikhs). Research suggest that religious beliefs are a central part of everyday life for ethnic groups, more than for the native white population of the UK. For example, Brierley (2013) found:

- *Worship.* Muslims (62%), Hindus (43%) and Black Christians (57%) are more likely to attend weekly worship compared to 37% of native white people,

- *Religiosity.* Muslims (74%), Hindus (43%) and Black Christians (81%) see their religion very important in their lives, more so than native white population (33%).

Modood et al (1997) found some decline in the importance of religion for all ethnic groups and that fewer were observant, especially among the second generation

However, such a sweeping generalisation is misleading as there are major differences between ethnic groups and their religiosity, some demonstrating more than others. found that religious beliefs are a central part of everyday life for ethnic minority groups, and more so then, for the native majority population of the UK. For example:

Reasons for minority ethnic groups being more religious

- **Socialisation.** Most immigrants had a high level of religious commitment before they entered the UK, and they have maintained this pattern in the UK. Davies (1994), a functionalist, argues that ethnic minority families such as Asian parents have socialised their younger generation to maintain a high level of religiosity by 'passing down' religious ideas and practises onto their children.

- **Religion and culture defence.** Bruce (2002) claims that religion provides ethnic minority groups a 'defence barrier' to preserve the ethnic group's identity when faced with hostility and racism from a dominating culture. Most British-born Muslims identify themselves essentially as Muslim or by their ethnic origin first, rather than by their British identity. For example, since the 11th September and 7th July terrorist attacks and the more recent attacks; Islamic communities have experienced a new wave of racism known as Islamophobia, which has brought more hostile attacks against individuals and mosques. This may explain the high level of support for Islam among young British Pakistanis, (e.g. girls wearing the 'hijab') who will often use their faith as a cultural identity in reaction against oppression, hatred and secular values in society.

For Afro-Caribbean Christians when they came over to the UK, they attempted to assimilate themselves in society. and incorporate themselves into mainstream white churches. Many found prejudice and racism towards them and did not welcome them. This led to the development of their own churches, e.g. the Pentecostal Church (a Christian sect). New immigrants often joined existing Christian churches such as Pentecostalism.

- **Cultural Transition. Bruce** (2002) also suggests that religion is used to help ethnic groups to make the transition for migrant group facing changes and adjustments to a new country or culture. Religious organisation provides a sense of community and support that helps people to cope with the changes. Modood et al (1994) found that religion was important in the lives of minority ethnic communities for socialisation and as means of maintaining traditional culture.

- **Economic and social deprivation.** Many immigrants coming to the UK tend to be poor and working class, and are looking for economic prosperity but often failed to achieve this. According to Stark and Bainbridge's (1985) **religious market theory** ethnic groups are more likely to be religious because they experience deprivation – socially (marginality) and economically (e.g. poverty). For this reason, they tend to show more religious beliefs and practises because it acts as a compensator for their deprived social and economic situation they find themselves in. Religion can bring social identity, status and sense of belonging, which may be lacking in mainstream society. This may explain why certain ethnic groups show high levels of religious behaviour, such Afro-Caribbean that practise Pentecostalism, Jehovah witness and Seventh-day Adventists,

Pakistani and Bangladeshi households are one of the poorest in the UK, about two-thirds of working age, are living in low-income households in 2014-2015. One explanation for the high religiosity for the Asian Muslim community, is if we apply Karl Max theory of religion. He saw religion as a 'drug for the working class people. This is because it provides a diversion from the real cause of their poverty and racial discrimination (i.e. the injustice of capitalist system) by providing comfort and compensation for their situation.

✓✗ Evaluation

> **✗ Religion is declining amongst all ethnic minorities**
>
> Although ethnic minorities may demonstrate higher level of religious beliefs and participation rates, but there has also been some decline in the importance of religion for all ethnic groups, especially amongst the second and third generation (children/grandchildren from original immigrant parents), which demonstrates each generation is become less religious then the previous one, which would support the secularisation theory.

> **✗ Socialisation not so important**
>
> The view that part of the reason for the high level of religiosity is due to socialisation has been questioned. Again (as stated above), there is a generation gap between first generation migrants and their third-generation grandchildren over religious issues (marriage, alcohol, dress code, attendance, beliefs etc.) which has resulted in conflict in parent-child relationship. Rather than becoming more religious, many children are now becoming more secular and have modified or rejected some of their parent's beliefs in order to fit into western culture.

> **✗ Marxism challenged**
>
> El-Saadawi has criticised the Marxist view of why religious beliefs in ethnicity minority is high. She argues that patriarchy and culture are more influential factors in shaping people's religious beliefs of ethnic minorities then poverty and the social class they are in.

Class and religiosity

There is not that much research into the relationship between social class and religious participation. This is because religions in the UK do not collect data about the occupational status of their congregations and the plethora of different types of new religious movement and new age tends to make it difficult to generalise about the relationship between class and religion. However, the research evidence that does exist suggests the following: the generalizations might be made:

- **Upper & middle classes:** Upper and middle classes dominate mainstream churches e.g. Anglican and Catholic congregations in the UK

- **Lower middle class & upper working class** dominate denominations congregations e.g. Methodism, Pentecostalism, Baptist as well as older, more established sects such as Mormons and Jehovah's Witnesses.

Mainstream church

Mainstream established Churches (e.g. Church of England) are dominated by the upper and upper-middle classes, especially women, tend to be over-represented in churches, though members of all social classes attend. This is supported by research surveys:

- An online survey by YouGov in 2015, of over 7000 adults, found that the upper and middle class are more like to go to church than the working classes; 62% of regular churchgoers were middle-class, whereas and only 38% were working class).

- A previous survey by British Social Attitudes (BSA) in 2012 found that 73% working class people (skilled manual workers) claimed they had never attended a religious service, compared with 63% middle-class people (professional and managerial workers). Ashworth and Farthing (2007) found that the poorest social groups, which are those people that were entirely dependent on state benefits for reasons such as sickness, unemployment or old age were the least likely social group to attend church.

Denominations

- Denomination (e.g. Methodist and Pentecostalism churches) tends to attract mainly skilled working-class people and lower middle class people. According to Ahern and Davie (1987) this is because working-class people are generally distrustful of institutions such as the Anglican Church (the state religion i.e. Church of England), which they see as hierarchical and too closely tied to the ruling elite (monarchy, the state and the establishment). They perceive mainstream religion as too formal, middle-class and authoritarian. working-class people were more heavily involved in non-conformist religions because these symbolised their contempt of the ruling establishment. This view is supported by Roy Wallis (1984) who argues that denominations tend to be slightly anti-establishment or non-conformist in character because they have broken away from the established Church of England. Such organisations are generally organised and run by their congregations.

- It could also be argued that the poorest socioeconomic groups may be attracted to Pentecostalism because of its 'theodicy of misfortune', which offers an explanation and a solution for their economic misfortune (e.g. Theodicies of misfortune tend to the belief that wealth and other manifestations of privilege are indications or signs of evil).

New Religious Movements & New Age Movements

- **Sects and cults (that are world-rejecting).** New religious movements (sects and cults) seems to attract people from the most deprived and marginal social groups. Sects Glock (1964) suggest the appeal of sects to some social groups is because of their experience of various types of deprivation in life, be it: social or economic. For example, poor working class people experience of economic deprivation may mean that they are (or were) attracted to sects (than middle-class) such as the Nation of Islam or Rastafarianisrn because these sects offer a means of coping with their disadvantage. They offer divine compensation for their low economic status. This ties in with Marxist's idea of religion acting as the 'opium of the people', or the Weberian idea of a theodicy of disprivilege). Weber argues that people need religion to help explain their lack of status in society. The working class are in the worst position, so religion is used to help deal with the fact that they are poor and marginalised.

- **Sects and cults (that are world-affirming).** Andrew Holden's (2002) suggest that some sects (which are world-affirming) are drawn from lower middle class, as well as the skilled working class such as Jehovah Witnesses. Attraction to sects from such social group are often as a result of some form of **spiritual deprivation** rather than economic deprivation. They have become unfulfilled or disillusioned with the social, political and economic system and seek alternative lifestyle. According to Bird (1999), world-affirming groups offer spiritual fulfilment, since the spiritual side of humanity has vanished to some extent from our rationalised and industrial world. For example, Wallis (xxxx) found that sects that appeared in the 1960s and 1970s such as the Children of God, the Jesus Army, the Unification Church and the International Society for Krishna Consciousness, attracted mainly middle-class, university-educated students who were experiencing spiritual deprivation. This means they felt disillusioned with the values of capitalist society and their parents' culture. As a result, they turned to these sects, which claimed to offer alternative spiritual fulfilment and enlightenment.

- Another explanation why some sects appeal to the education/middle-class maybe due to **ethical deprivation.** This explanation may explain the attraction of Islamic fundamentalism to some members of the young, upwardly-mobile Muslim middle class. Bruce (2002) argues that university-educated young Muslims may feel that the Western capitalist system is too dependent on materialism and is therefore spiritually corrupt. They may be attracted to Islamism because this fundamentalist movement stresses a return to what they see as traditional values. It therefore represents an attempt to reclaim the past and attain a sense of certainty in an uncertain world.

- **New Age Movements.** Many new age movements (e.g. ideas/spirituality) seem to appeal mainly to the young middle class, notably they tend to educated and female. The ages that participate are fairly evenly represented, the highest percentage being 42% in the 35-49 age group. One explanation is the cost of investing in these spiritual interests and personal development can be quite high. Bruce (1995) suggest new religious movements appeal to the young affluent and professional middle class who are generally successful wealthy, but would like to fill a spiritual void, or need self-improvement, such as becoming more successful in their working and personal lives. Heelas (1996) suggest yoga, meditation and spiritual healing appeal mainly to middle-class women than men. who have a deep interest in exploring their full potential Interesting to note, astrology and fortune-telling appeal more to working-class women.

✓✗ Evaluation

> **✗ Working class just as religious**
>
> There is research evidence that does not support the view that middle class are more religious than the working class. Lawes (2009) found that the working class, especially the uneducated are more likely to maintain their religious beliefs throughout their lives (known as lifelong theists) than middle class. This contradicts the findings relating to church attendance, which found middle class more likely to attend.

> **✗ Church attendance**
>
> Although research evidence suggests that the working class may not attended religious service as much as middle class, this does not mean they are any less religious or subscribe to atheist ideas. Rather, it can indicate that working-class people are apathetic about or uninterested in religion because it offers no meaningful contribution to their daily lives. It therefore, may support Grace Davie's (1994) "believing without belonging" hypothesis.

> **✗ Other factors involved**
>
> Sociologists need to be cautious when generalising about the link between church attendance and social class. This is because other factors such as 'immigration' may distort statistics which will lead to a different conclusion about class and religion attendance. For example, there is evidence that church attendance in deprived inner city areas of large cities is higher than in urban areas. This is because immigrants to the UK are relatively poor working-class people who, tend to have a deeper religious faith than the majority white population, are disproportionately likely to live in these areas. This explains the high turnout in inner city churches (e.g. Methodist, Pentecostal and Baptist churches).

> **✗ Marxist view challenged**
>
> The Marxist view that working class are attracted to religion because it offers an explanation and a solution for their economic misfortune has been challenged by neo-Marxist. Maduro, a neo-Marxists suggest that religion may also appeal to the poorest social classes to fight their oppression, as in liberation theology in South America.

Age and religiosity

In general, the relationship between age and religious attendance in the UK demonstrates:

Attendance

- The churchgoers tend to be much older (between 55-65 years old) than those who do not attend, with one exception; those under the age of 15 years of age, who are more likely to go than any other age group above them. However, the under 15 yrs category does not signify a strong religious commitment but is more based around religious functions such as Sunday schools and 'tagging along with parents'. This suggest that people seem to develop a greater attachment to religion as they grow older.

- According to Brierley (2015) church attendance is falling in all age groups (age groups: under 15; 20-29; 30—44; 45-64; 65 and over) apart from those aged over 65 years of age. Since the 1980s the number of young people going to church is decreasing rapidly and this trend is projected to continue to fall.

Beliefs

- A YouGov (2015) poll found that belief in God is lowest among those under 40 years of age, and highest among those over age 55. According to Voas (2008), people born before 1945 are more likely to say they believe that God exists or that they still believe in God, despite having doubts, compared to people born after 1975, who were twice as likely as the older group to state they did not believe in God.

Sociological explanations for greater religiosity among the older generation

Voas and Crockett (2005) suggest three possible explanations for the age difference in religious beliefs/practices:

- **The ageing effect.** The ageing effect is the view that people turn to religion as they become older. As people approach death, they 'naturally' become more concerned about spiritual matters such as the afterlife. As a result, they are more likely to go to church.

- **Disengagement.** This is the view that people become detached from society as they get older. For example, retirement from work and the death of family, friends and relatives can often result in social isolation and loneliness. One way to compensate is to participation in a religion, because religious organisations offer integration into a community offering social and emotional supports.

- **The generational effect.** The generational effect is the view that each new generation is less religious than the one before, as society becomes more secular.

Explanations for the lack of young people's belief

- **Religion is not appealing to the young.** Brierley (2002) research survey found that 87% of 10 to 14-year-olds thought church was unattractive because it boring, repetitive and, old fashioned and full of old people that are out of touch with the styles and attitudes of young people. Furthermore, controversial issues in religion such as abortion, contraception, gay rights, sex before marriage, and the ordination of women priests, etc. seem bizarre and alien to the values they young people hold.

- **Pragmatic reasons.** There are also practical explanations for the decline of religious belief and commitment among the young population. Brierley (2002) also found that the young have greater demand on their time compared to people from the previous generations. Leisure pursuits play a much bigger part of people's life now than before; with shops, clubs and pubs all open for very long hours, including on Sundays, the young simply have more interesting and enjoyable things to do then go to church.

- **Individualisation.** Britain has increasingly become an individualistic culture, which means individual now demonstrate greater independence in mental and social behaviour, rather conforming to social rules and constraints that young people in the past felt compelled to follow religious rules. Catto (2014) suggests young people are more likely to rely on their own consciences, rather than religious rules, to guide their behavior.

- **Secularization.** As religion declines in society and with the decline of religious socialisation in the family and educational system, coupled with the fact that schools now engage in a generalised secular or moral education, or ignore it altogether. This means that the majority of young people will become more disengaged from religion, but it may also reflect the fact that most of them don't require it.

- **The decline of metanarratives.** Postmodernist sociologists such as like Lyotard (1984) argue that young people are more likely to feel disenchanted with the world because metanarratives (grand theories) like religion has lost the power to explain how the world works; it has lost its influential appeal. This is because the impact of globalisation has opened up the easy access to an number of variety of other alternative explanations of how the world works, most notably scientific explanations.

- **The privatization of belief.** Young people may be choosing to treat their religion, of whatever faith or mix of beliefs, as a private matter. Even if they have some general spiritual or religious beliefs, they may not feel they belong to any particular religion, or are committed to any specific religious doctrine. They may prefer not to make any public display of whatever they believe through involvement in religious organizations, or admit to them in surveys. Davie (1994) expressed this in the words 'believing without belonging'.

- **Increased spiritual choice.** Lynch (2008) suggests that young people are turning away from conventional ideas of religion because young people today are exposed to a wider diversity of ideas and practices than previous generations. In addition to conventional mainstream religion, alternative spiritual beliefs and philosophical ideas such as atheism, paganisms, vampirism, Goth culture, humanism, existentialism, rationalism and so on. Roof (2001) calls this an expanded spiritual marketplace. These have opened up new avenues for exploring religion and spirituality. Lynch suggests that these have meant there are now more sources for young people can pick 'n' mix on religious and spiritual beliefs to form identities and lifestyles. This means young people are finding expression outside traditional religions and religious organizations.

✓✗ Evaluation

✗ Elderly losing their faith

There is research evidence that shows the elderly are also losing their belief which contradicts other research findings, which suggest that the faith remains strong (e.g. such as Voas study, 2008). A longitudinal survey of retired people conducted over 20 years found that the elderly are losing faith in God. A number of the participants attributed their declining faith to disappointment with churches and the clergy. They cited insensitive handling of bereavement, the 'self-importance' of some clergy members and a lack of interest in the elderly (Coleman, 2000).

✗ A critique of ageing effect explanation

A criticism of Voas and Crockett ageing effect explanation which states that people turn to religion as they get older because they are attracted to religion, may only be partially correct. It could be argued that older people grew up at a time when religion was more popular. When they were young, it was the norm to attend church. Their greater church attendance, therefore, merely reflects old habits.

✗ Privatized beliefs of the young

The view that the young are less religious has been challenged. The fact that the young do not attend church services or religious practice, does not necessarily mean that young people are lacking in religious feeling and belief. Being religious may be viewed as being very 'uncool' in many young peer groups eyes, which exerts social pressure not to be religious. This will consequently mean for some young people their beliefs will be expressed privately for a while, which are difficult to record in statistical survey, and thus may explain to some extent, the low rates of religiosity of the young.

Exam Questions

1. Outline and explain **two** ways in which women may be disadvantaged by religion today. . . . . . .[10 marks]

2. Outline and explain **two** reasons why some people from ethnic groups seem to participate more in religious activity than other social groups. . . . .[10 marks]

3. Applying material from **Item...** analyse **two** differences between the religious beliefs and participation of your people compared with those of older people. . . . .[10 marks]

4. Applying material from **Item...** and your knowledge, evaluate the relationship between gender and religious belief and practice. . . . .[20 marks]

5. Applying material from **Item...** and your knowledge, evaluate sociological explanations for the view that, for minority ethnic groups, the practice of religion and membership of religious groups is mainly a form of cultural defence. . . . .[20 marks]

The AQA specification:

- Ideology, science and religion, including both Christian and non-Christian religious traditions.

The exam requires that you are able to:

▶ Understand and evaluate the different definitions of 'religion'.

▶ Understand and explain the difference between 'science; and 'religion' as belief systems.

▶ Evaluate 'science' and 'religion' as beliefs systems.

▶ Understand and evaluate the different types of 'ideology' as a belief system.

Key terms

- **Belief systems** are a set of ideas through which an individual believed to be true. Belief systems aim to makes sense of the world around us. There are two forms such belief systems: open belief system tends to be *evidence-based* and closed belief system tends to be *faith-based*. Religion and science are referred to as belief systems as they attempt to explain how the world works.

- **Religion** is a beliefs system set of ideas and beliefs relating to the supernatural e.g. belief in a God or entity of some kind, which ultimately provides a sense of meaning and a means of interpreting and explaining the world. Religion tend to be *faith-based*: a strong sense of trust and conviction in the God/entity, which is not based on observable and testable evidence

- **Science** refers to the *method* of gathering information empirically (scientific method i.e. experimentations and observations) that provides valid and reliable knowledge about the world. Science also refers to particular body of knowledge gathered using the scientific method (e.g. Physics, biology and chemistry). The aim of science is to understand, explain, predict and where possible to control the world around us.

- **Ideology.** The term 'ideology' refers to a particular vision or way of seeing the world or having a set of ideas and values. Ideology can be seen as a form of belief systems held by an individual, a group or society. There are different types of ideologies, many important ones tend to be political/economical/social (e.g. Conservativism, Anarchism, capitalism, Marxism and feminisms) or religious beliefs (e.g. Christianity, Buddhism). Often ideologies are held to justify their interest of particular social or political groups – to their benefit.

The debate – issues of defining religion

These exam notes firstly deal with the definition of religion. As you will see there are different way of defining religion. How we define it is important, as the definition decide what determine what can be classified as a religious and what should not, whether society is becoming more or less religious or whether religious belief is simply changing the forms it takes. There are three main ways that sociologists define religion, substantive, functional and social constructionist

Substantive and exclusivist definition

- **Belief in the supernatural.** Substantive definition focuses on the actual 'features' of what makes up a religion (think 'substance' for 'substantive') e.g. belief in God, religious teachings and practises –required and heaven, hell, worship and prayer, the afterlife. Max Weber (1905) defines religion, one that must include in the belief in God or the supernatural power that cannot be explained scientifically. Substantive definitions are **exclusive**; they draw a clear line between religious and non-religious beliefs; if there is no idea of a 'God' within the religion then it is not a religion. This definition leaves no room for beliefs of practices that perform similar functions to religion but do not involve belief in god. This definition fits with what must people would regard as religion, such as Christianity, Judaism and Islam.

- **Relating to the sacred.** An alternative substantive definition is providing by Durkheim (1912), who defines religion by distinguishing between the sacred and the profane. Sacred can include anything that people perceives as being sacred that evoke awe, reverences or has a special meaning. Sacred things can be anything such as beliefs, practices, objects, buildings, places, events and time. Profane is everyday activity that does not have any significance or meaning. For example, a candle lit at home because of a power-cut is 'profane', but becomes 'sacred' when it is lit in church for the soul of loved ones.

- Sociologist that follow the 'substantive and exclusivist' definition such as Giddens (2006), defines religion as 'shared beliefs and rituals that provide a sense of ultimate meaning and purpose by creating an idea of reality that is sacred, all-encompassing and supernatural'. Main features (but not all) under this definition include:

  - *Belief in the supernatural:* beliefs in the supernatural e.g. belief in a God, gods, a person or being of some kind, which ultimately provides a sense of meaning and a means of interpreting and explaining the world

  - *Faith-based:* a strong sense of trust and conviction in the God/entity, which is not based on observable, testable or falsifiable evidence.

  - *An unchanging truth:* religions usually contain certain fundamental and unchangeable beliefs, like Christ being the son of God, or Mohammed being Allah's Prophet.

  - *Theology:* a set of teachings, usually based on some holy book, such as the Bible.

  - *Practice:* a series of rituals or ceremonies to express religious beliefs, either publicly or privately e.g. praying, and fasting.

  - *Institutions:* some place of organization (e.g. church) and with some form of hierarchy of status (priest)

  - *Morals:* a set of moral to guide or influence the everyday behaviour of believers

Functional and inclusive definition

- Some sociologist such as Emile Durkheim (1915) defines religion in terms of the social or psychological functions can perform for individuals or society; rather than to any specific God or the supernatural. For example, religion helps encourage 'social unity' by instilling the same values with each other's, which helps integrate societies or groups of people together. Milton Yinger 1970 identifies functions that religion performs for individuals, such as help answer questions about the meaning of existence and what happens after when we die. The functional definition is seen as **inclusive**, as it tends to leave the definition of religion broad (for inclusive, think of ' all Including') as it allows any wide range of beliefs and practices that has a positive psychological/social or functions for society and individuals.

Social constructionist definitions

- **Social constructionists** are interested in how definitions of religion are 'constructed' by people. They believe religions are social created by society by powerful social groups or people. More importantly Social constructionists are interested in how definitions of religion are constructed, challenged and fought over. For example, functionalist, such Emile Durkheim take the view that there is not such thing as a divine God or the supernatural and are a product of humans in order to bring people together to share a common group identity, that distinguishes them from other. Marxists, on the other hand, such as Karl Marx sees religion created to justify power inequalities between the classes- ruling class and the working class. Alan Aldridge (2013) shows how powerful groups in society can benefit, deny or modify religious beliefs systems. For example, many governments such Germany, Belgium and Russian have banned or refused to recognise 'scientology' with a legal status as a religion. Or another example, is how is some Islamic countries 'apostasy', conversion to another religion or the renunciation of Islam is a crime punishable by death e.g. Saudi Arabia or Pakistan as an example.

✓✗ Evaluation

Substantive/exclusive definition

✗ **Too exclusive**

One problem with the substantive/exclusivists definition of religion is that in order to be defined as a religion it must include supernatural element such as the belief in God. The problem with this definition this will exclude some religions do not believe or make reference to a God, e.g. Buddhism or Confucianism. This means some sociologists dismissive the substantive definition as it can be too exclusive.

✗ **'Supernatural problematic word'**

A further problem with the substantive/exclusivists definition of religion is that the term 'supernatural' can be problematic. It is not clear what can be and cannot be defined as 'supernatural' and subsequently which be classified as a 'religion' and which are not. For example, UFOs, astrology, witchcraft would be considered as religions under this definition.

✗ **Problem was the concept sacred**

Another problem is Durkheim's view of the sacred. This has been criticised for being too broad which can include belief system that many not regard as religious. For example, communism, nationalism, football team, music band, the lives of celebrities and royalty can take on an almost sacred quality for some people, and play a similar role in their lives as some conventional religions. For example, a football teams' colours or a nation's flag can be defined sacred – regarded with respect and devotion.

Functional/inclusive definition

✗ **Too broad a definition**

The functional/inclusive definitions have also been criticised for being too wide as a definition. Such a definition would include belief systems such as communism, nationalism, and sports such football teams, where shared beliefs and rituals also encourage a sense of 'unity' amongst believers. For example, this means some sociologists are dismissive of the functional definition as it can be too broad and include belief system that many will not view as a religion.

Religion and science

Religion and science are referred to as belief systems as they attempt to explain how the world works. Dixon (2008) observes that until approximately 200 years ago, religion and modern science were not separate and distinct types of knowledge but were seen primarily as one. This is because science was dominated by religious thinkers who believed that the primary purpose of science was to document the glory of God, such as did Newton.

Dixon notes that modern science grew and became separate from religion in the 18th century Europe, during a period known as the Enlightenment. This was a time were a shift in thinking in explaining the unknown and the world around us – towards a rational and logical thinking process based on empirical evidence (facts and observations). Notably it was a time when Darwin published his evolutionary theory in his book called, 'On the Origin of Species', in 1859, that conflicted with religious views about how the world, animals and human had evolved. Therefore, religious belief systems of how the natural world works were largely superseded by scientific belief systems during the Enlightenment period.

The differences between religion and science

Science is an 'open belief system'

Dixon compared the belief systems of science and religion and identified the following differences between them; notably science is referred to as being an 'open belief system' and religion as being a 'closed belief system'. Karl

✗ Science not always an open system

The view that science is an open belief system has been challenged by Feyerabend (1975). He argues that science is not as open as it claims because what scientists say what they do is often different from what they actually do. Individual scientists follow their own rules and often deviate from rational thinking and practices; there is no such thing as a scientific method that all scientists faithfully follow.

✗ Scientific theories not always based on evidence

The view that science is an evidence-based as opposed to faith-based has been challenged. Lakatos (1974) argues how science is practised is not always based on evidence. Scientific knowledge does not always grow in a cumulative manner based on evidence (using the falsification principle). According to Lakatos, in reality the process of investigation or knowledge are often by accident, luck, inspired guesswork and imagination (made up data)- in other words, the rules in science is that "anything goes", not the open system of how science is believed to work.

✗ Peer review is not fool proof

There has been debate as to how effective the peer review process really is in scrutinising and criticising scientific knowledge. Kaplan (1964) argues when scientists submit their research paper for peer review in the scientific journals may not be 'value-free' as they can often 'fabricate/fictionalize' their findings. If a scientist knowingly and deliberately sets out to plagiarise or falsify data, a team of reviewers may not be able to detect it. According to Kaplan cheating is fairly commonplace in science because scientists are heavily biased towards proving their own theories right. There is little chance of being caught because there is no prestige in re-doing someone else's work, meaning that little attempt is made to replicate and verify the work of other scientists.

✗ The stability of Beliefs.

Michael Polanyi (1958) article *The Stability of Beliefs* argues that science is not as open to scrutiny from other scientists as suggested by Popper, but can often been seen as close-belief system, similar to religion. This is because any evidence that is contradictory to any of their belief, they employ techniques to protect them from the contradiction such as 'circular false reasoning, and ad hoc explanations ('afterwards' explanation is given to explain away any contradiction). For example, if a religious prayer that does not work this may be explained away by "God is testing your faith", etc. In this way, he claims all beliefs be it science or religion remain stable – protected any challenges - protected.

✗ Scientific knowledge is socially constructed.

Interpretivist sociologists argue that scientific knowledge is socially constructed. They argue that 'science' does not tell us 'the truth' but offer one of potentially many explanations for understanding the world. Michel Foucault (1977) argues that scientific knowledge is produced by social groups often those who have power – knowledge and power are tightly interwoven. He argues that scientific knowledge can be used as a tool by the powerful to legitimates scientific knowledge in ways that best serves their interests. For example, the "climate change denial movement"— despite the scientific evidence showing climate change's dangerous outcomes, powerful interests suppressed this knowledge by introducing doubt about climate change, which they backed up using a scientific knowledge. Michel Foucault argues that powerful interest's groups created the illusion that a scientific debate was taking place when, in reality, there wasn't, demonstrating how scientific belief can be socially manipulated.

✗ The overlap between science and religion

It can be argued that science resembles religion in many ways and that there are more similarities than differences. For example, they both contain 'saints' and 'priests' a collection of people, usually men, who are revered and whose teachings or views are regarded as sacred and rarely questioned. The writings of these scientific saints and priests have a 'holy' status in the scientific community.

Ideology

Like religion and science, ideology also offers a means of interpreting and explaining the world. However, ideology differs from religion in that ideologies are not necessarily based on faith in supernatural beliefs but are held by a social group to benefit in some way such as socially, politically or economically. Below we examine the 'nature' and 'role' of ideology through three different perspectives: scientism, Marxism and feminism (themselves an ideology). We look at what they have to say about ideology in the context of society, science and religion.

Scientism: science ideology

- Science is an ideology because it believes it can explain, control and predict the world we live in using the scientific methods. An extreme view is called **scientism**. This ideology claims 'only scientific knowledge is valid' and that gaining genuine true knowledge about the world, can only be based purely on a strict commitment to empirical evidence achieved by only using the scientific method of investigation. Any other forms of knowledge gathered by adhering to the strict methods of scientific investigation cannot be trusted.

  - *Religion* – It rejects unequivocally any alleged truths and claims to knowledge that cannot be explained empirically tested using the scientific method, such as those provided by religions, parapsychology, sociology and philosophy. Scientism may be regarded as another form of ideology, protecting and justifying the interests of scientists which is often to dismiss competing ideologies such as religion.

Marxism: dominant ideology and hegemony

- **Dominant ideology.** According to Marxists, ideology are ideas of particular social groups that reflects their interests. Marxists believe that the ideas that people hold about society are formed by what position in their social class they are in. He argues that there is one *dominant ideology* which is held by the most powerful groups society, which reflects the ruling class views of society. Althusser (1971) believes that the dominant ideology are transmitted and spread using *ideological state apparatuses*; these are social institutions like the family, the education system, the media, the law and religion, which justified the power of the dominant social class.

Mannheim (1936) argues that the dominant social groups protect their 'dominant Ideology' by distorting/obscuring the facts in order to hide the inequalities of capitalist society in order to continue privileged position of the dominant class; dominating society, and to prevent any social change that might threaten their interests.

- **Hegemony.** Gramsci (1971) further developed the Marxist view of ideology with his concept of hegemony. *Hegemony* refers to the how the dominant ideology, maintains its power or control through ideas rather than simply through coercion (force). It does this by persuading other social classes, and particularly the working class, by socializing them into ruling-class ideology and this making them believing it is also part of their beliefs and values that they hold. Hegemony prevents the working class become aware of the reality of their inequality and exploitation (class consciousness), which prevents them from overthrowing the dominant class by revolution in order to create a classless communist society.

  - *Religion* – in terms of religion Marxist, see religion as part of the ideology of the dominant class in society to helping to justify the interests of that class. For example, Karl Max saw religious ideology as an 'opium', a drug for the working class because it provides a comforting diversion (e.g. eternal afterlife, making poverty bearable by justifying happiness in the afterlife) from seeing the real cause of their poverty—the injustice of capitalist system.

  - *Science* – in terms of science, Marxists see science as an ideology that works in favour of powerful group. They argue that many advances in the name of 'pure' science have actually been driven by profit and power by the dominate social groups in society. For example, scientific advancement in agriculture such genetically-modified seeds that resist insects and herbicides, benefit agribusiness and food transnationals companies rather than the people of the developing world. This is because these Western companies control the cost and distribution of seeds, fertilisers and pesticides and they rather develop and sell their product to rich western countries.

Feminism and ideology

- **Patriarchal ideology** Feminists see society dominated by a *patriarchal ideology*, which is a set of ideas that supports and tries to justify the male dominance in society. Patriarchal ideology is the beliefs that men are superior, more logical and less emotional than women. Women are seen as being more suited to childcare and family tasks rather than responsible positions requiring measured, unemotional and logical qualities. Patriarchal ideology has lead to gender inequality in society; women being in a subordinate position to men in all areas.

  - *Religion* – in terms of religion, feminist see religious beliefs and practises reflecting a patriarchal ideology; seeing women as being inferior to men. This has led to gender inequality and legitimates female subordination in society (e.g. family, motherhood roles). For example, [1] high-status positions within traditional religious organisation and are often led by men; [2] Muslim and Jewish women are prohibited in women are also prohibited from reading their holy scriptures or entering the place of worship when menstruating as this is regarded as unclean/impure; [3] the female body in religious scriptures are often portrayed as a sexual temptress and sinful distraction, leading men astray which needs to be controlled e.g. veiling of women in Islam.

  - *Science* – in terms of science, history often been excluded women from scientific institutions. Pauline Marks (1979) describes how science was used to justify patriarchal ideology which led to the exclusion of women from education until the 19305. Male doctors, scientists and educationalists in this period often expressed the view that the education of females would lead to the creation of "a new race of puny and unfeminine" females and "disqualify women from their true vocation", namely the nurturing of the next generation. Ann Oakley (1972) describes the psychology theory of 'maternal deprivation'. The view that it is harmful to the child to be continuously separated from its mother, could result in long term cognitive, social, and emotional difficulties later on in life. The maternal theory appeared in the 1950s, as a scientific ideology that justified men dominating paid work while women stayed at home to raise children.

✓✗ Evaluation

Science ideology

> ✗ **Scientism too simplistic and reductionist**
>
> Most scientists do not subscribe to scientism and many do not accept that science is the only means of understanding the world. This is because reducing the world we live in to only thinks that can only test by observable ignores, the cultural, social, historical, psychological and philosophical aspect. For example, science cannot adequately explain psychological disorder such as eating disorders, phobias, depression or how to deal with bereavement or divorce. It cannot explain historical and social aspect of life e.g. World Wars I and II, Henry the III V, racism, sexism and so on. Many scientists themselves hold religious beliefs about the world and the meaning of life, representing the spiritual dimensions of their lives, alongside their attempts to use science to understand the world.

> ✗ **The contradiction of scientism**
>
> Scientism is often used to debunk parapsychology and religious beliefs; anything that cannot be proven by using the empirical methods such as observation and experimentation. However, there is no scientific experiment to prove that religious beliefs e,g, such as God does not exist., Despite this, they continue to deny the existence of God without any real scientific proof e.g. via observation or experimentation; the very methods method they argue is the only true way!

Marxist ideology

> ✗ **Hegemony questioned**
>
> The Marxist view that hegemony (ideology) prevents the working class prevents them from overthrowing the capitalism has been questioned. It could be argued it may not be this ideology that prevents attempts to overthrow capitalism but economic factors such as fear of losing their jobs that keeps workers from rebelling against the capitalist system

✗ Religion in decline

The decline of religious beliefs means religious ideology acting as a form of controlling factor may no longer be applicable if people don't believe in religion any more. This suggest that Marxist theory religion as part of the ideology of the dominant class in society to helping to justify the interests of that class may not be valid any more.

Feminist ideology

✗ Feminist ideology questioned

Not all religions support a patriarchal ideology. Women are now taking up positions of authority e.g. Pentecostal and Anglican churches, and the Church of England has allowed female vicars since 1992. Reformed Judaism has allowed women to become rabbis since 1972. Arguably, Buddhism have never been oppressive to women.

✗ Science still a male dominated ideology

Although more women do enter science, this would suggest that the ideology of science has adjusted and that institutions of science are gender-neutral meritocracy. However, this is questioned when women fail to climb the scientific hierarchy, it is suggested that there are innate sex-linked differences in talent (e.g. superior mathematical skills of men). Research suggests that patriarchal prejudice and discrimination continue to be responsible for gender inequalities in science employment.

Exam Questions

1. Outline and explain **two** ways in which religious interpretations of the world might differ from scientific ones.. . . . .[10 marks]

2. Outline and explain **two** criticisms of the view that science is an open system. . . . .[10 marks]

3. Outline and explain **two** limitations of the functionalist view of religion. . . . .[10 marks]

4. Applying material from **Item...** analyse **two** differences between religion and ideology belief systems. . . . .[10 marks]

5. Applying material from **Item...** and your knowledge, evaluate sociological explanations of the nature and role of ideology. . . . .[20 marks]

6. Applying material from **Item...** and your knowledge, evaluate the view that science has replaced religion as a main influence on people's knowledge and beliefs in society today.. . .[20 marks]

7. Applying material from **Item...** and your knowledge, evaluate the view that religion is still the most significant ideological influence in the world today.. . . . .[20 marks]

9 781906 468545